Break the Rules, Destroy Toxic Habits, and Have the Best Sex of Your Life

Dr. Chris Donaghue, PhD

RUNNING PRESS

PHILADELPHIA

Running Press
Hachette Book Group
1290 Avenue of the Americas, New York, NY 10104
www.runningpress.com
@Running_Press

Printed in the United States of America

First Edition: January 2019

Published by Running Press, an imprint of Perseus Books, LLC, a subsidiary of Hachette Book Group, Inc. The Running Press name and logo is a trademark of the Hachette Book Group.

The Hachette Speakers Bureau provides a wide range of authors for speaking events. To find out more, go to www.hachettespeakersbureau.com or call (866) 376-6591.

The publisher is not responsible for websites (or their content) that are not owned by the publisher.

Print book cover and interior design by Josh McDonnell.

Library of Congress Control Number: 2018952000

ISBNs: 978-0-7624-6533-0 (paperback), 978-0-7624-6534-7 (ebook)

LSC-C

10   9   8   7   6   5   4   3   2   1

CONTENTS

FOREWORD BY AMBER ROSE

And just like that, we became best friends. Unorthodox in many ways, my friendship with Dr. Chris blossomed over the mic. We patiently listened to one another's perspectives as Dr. Chris explored, delicately yet fearlessly, the prevailing theories on sex positivity, love, and relationships.

It's rare to find a companion who aligns so closely with one's personal mission, and it's an honor to have Dr. Chris by my side as a boundless rebel of thought, a "work husband," and a forever friend.

Together we've inspired, transformed, and pushed each other forward as we've worked to dismantle and challenge the problematic forces that oppress people's true sexualities. As a feminist and social justice advocate, Dr. Chris works tirelessly to challenge slut-shaming and sexism, help put an end to rape culture, and support underacknowledged voices.

We spend so much time and energy trying to be different from who we really are and struggling to conform to others' expectations. We believe we need to be who we are *told* to be. But by following other people's rules, we only end up disguising and disowning our most beautiful, special parts.

Rebel Love, like all of Dr. Chris's work, helps to liberate and heal us from falsehoods with a sex-positive and compassionate approach. Live the message of *Rebel Love*, and live honest and proud as whoever and whatever you may be. Dr. Chris reminds us that it's okay to be you, whatever that may look like right now.

—Amber Rose

ACKNOWLEDGMENTS

This book would not have been possible without the people who have lifted me up, inspired and transformed me, and at times just sat with me when I thought I couldn't push forward. It's often the more subtle support that creates the needed foundation to do something like write a book.

To all the rebels and radicals who live bravely outside the box, always loudly pushing forward when the world says to conform and to be silent and small: you are all my heroes.

Thanks to Conner Habib, one of the smartest human beings I know: your brilliance and deep care and thoughtfulness inspire me, but also model for me what truth and full authenticity would look like were I to ever fully get there. You live your life so honestly, and that continues to make me feel less alone in all this. Your mere presence transforms me. More thanks than I could express.

Deep thanks to Ron Robbins, for doing the emotional labor of both making me laugh when needed and calling me out when I think I know it all. Your love and friendship is definitely part of the bedrock for the creation of this book. You have far more creativity and power than you realize, and I'm thankful you share that with me.

I am grateful to Tim Lewis, my friend and also a brilliant writer. You are always a safe, smart, and thoughtful mind to turn to when I'm struggling or needing inspiration. Thanks for continuing to fight the battle alongside me and never tiring. You carry a big heart and remind me to always show up with mine.

I have to thank Wesley Woods, always a superstar to me, who loved me even when I couldn't love myself. It's been a journey of growth and pain, but so full of beauty, too. Thanks for loving all of me, especially my less lovable and complicated parts. We took on the world together, and we continue to do so now in our own ways. Always in my heart.

Thanks to my work wife, Amber Rose, one of the strongest women I know, who moves through the world with power and so much compassion. You have taught me how to build a career that I can be proud of with strength while also using so much heart.

I thank my mom and brothers: in a world where so many lack a tight family unit of support, I'm blessed to have you three. Though geographically far away, you are all always close when I need you. Mom, your presence and continued love of this punchy radical keeps me feeling held in love and motivation. Thanks for always understanding and pushing me forward. Jay, the other most intelligent person I know, thanks for stepping up and stepping in; otherwise we would all drift. You are an anchor, and so loved for it. You have always loved me, all of me. Tim, you colorful and wild radical. You also show me what truth and authenticity look like. The world demands conformity, and you throw up the finger and live your truth. So much love to you.

To have that one person who is always so excited to hear everything that is happening in your life is one of the greatest gifts. My dad is that gift, and I still think to call him each time something exciting happens for me. Looking back now, I can see how his full love and support for everything I did not only saved me but also empowered me. I know you are still beside me and cheering me on. Miss you.

Harriet Duncan, my great friend and publicist extraordinaire, thanks for always having my back, whether it's with love or career, for being my date to events, and for always believing in me.

Thanks to my cowriter, Laura Barcella. Your wit, humor, and artistry shaped my ramblings into an actual readable book. Working with you has been a seamless gift. I'm grateful that you dived into my mind, work, and politics with deep respect and helped me make something that I hope can help heal the world a bit. I'm so thankful to have had you with me on this journey.

To my agent, Brandi Bowles, deep thanks for taking me on. The bumpy road of trying to get this book together ended as soon as you entered the process. You know your stuff, and you delivered. This wouldn't have been possible without you. It's a gift to be able to let go and trust that those on your side truly are. I look forward to more.

It's fair to say that a lot of the credit for getting this book published belongs to Tina Dunca. Thank you for helping this book land in Brandi's hands and for always showing up with all you have to help me. I'm moved by your interest and continued support of my work.

Thanks to Jordana Tusman and Running Press for taking me and my work on and for seeing the value in my mission. To find a home for your book where you feel fully accepted and celebrated is a huge blessing. I love what we have developed together and am grateful for your support in getting it out there.

INTRODUCTION

Everything you've been taught about sex and dating is wrong. All those dating rules from your therapist; all your friends' well-meaning suggestions about when to text, call, or sleep with a new partner; and most of the dating books on shelves today are wrong. While most dating books are well intentioned and try to be helpful, they are actually full of advice that both counsels you *away* from being your true, authentic self and reinforces sexist gender values.

I want to help fix this. For more than fifteen years, I've earned my clients' trust as a certified sex therapist with a strong personal connection to left-of-center, misunderstood, and marginalized communities. These are among the hundreds of thousands of people who follow me and listen to me on *The Amber Rose Show with Dr. Chris* (formerly *Loveline)*, the popular podcast I cohost with Amber Rose.

Rebel Love is a different kind of sex and dating book. It focuses on how to be genuine and self-accepting, not how to be respectable, classy, or a "lady." Healthy relationships ignore gender roles (and gender altogether) and focus instead on desire and compassion; they're about expression and freedom, not regulation and control.

What needs to be addressed is not how to catch a man or woman or how to be "better" in bed, but rather how to build authenticity from the inside out, gain appreciation for body and sex positivity, eliminate the harmful practice of slut-shaming both in your own life and in wider society, and bring an end to rape culture.

Most dating advice is outdated and oppressive. I want this to be a book for the rest of us: the smart, informed, open-minded masses who sense that traditional sex and dating norms are repressing us, but want to go beyond simply acknowledging this and actually *do something to change it*. Together, let's turn all the old-fashioned sex and dating rules that are harming our relationships *and* our culture on their heads.

I want to show you how to make your sex life hotter and your relationships healthier (and no, those two goals aren't mutually exclusive), no matter where you fall on the gender or sexual identity scale. To help combat the toxic messaging we've been steeped in all our lives, I'm presenting a whole new set of touchstones, some of which may be controversial or unfamiliar to you. Let's take a look.

People are diverse and it's time to embrace that.

This book is for everyone: all genders, races, ages, backgrounds, sexualities, and body types. (People who body-shame don't want a partner; they want a fantasy. If you complain about the size of your partner's penis, go buy a dildo—you aren't ready for a real relationship.) I'm in support of redefining gender, embracing all kinds of sex, killing stereotypes, and empowering people to be who they are, both in and out of the bedroom.

There are no more dating rules or sex rules, period.

This means no ego-based lists of dream-partner requirements, no more "should I or shouldn't I?" texting games, no more setting limits on who you'll date or have sex with. I advocate for doing what feels right, even if that's texting her five minutes after you've met, having sex with him on the first date, or trying any consensual type of kink, fantasy, or nontraditional relationship that turns you on.

Self-acceptance is everything.

This means learning to radically accept not just your body but your mind and your sexual desires. It's not about being classy, appropriate, on-trend, IG popular, or "respectable." I don't believe in changing who you are; this book is about choosing not to cooperate with ageism, thinspiration, slut-shaming, body-shaming, and so on.

Anonymous sex can be a relationship in and of itself.

One-night stands can be just as valuable, intimate, and transformative as years-long relationships. I differ from most conventional therapists out there in that I encourage people to have lots of sex with lots of people. Why? Because it helps you connect with others *and* yourself.

Self-help is selfish.

As a culture, we're overly focused on individualism and self, often forgetting that we grow most within relationships. Plus, we are *always* in relationships (even when we're alone, we are still emotionally and psychologically connected to people). I encourage people to focus on relational help, not self-help, and relational esteem, not self-esteem—think *we*, not me.

Your sexuality is fluid.

How you identify now isn't necessarily how you will identify for the rest of your life. Though sexual fluidity has been getting more public recognition in the past few years, there are other sexual identities still commonly neglected; for example, asexuals and solosexuals (asexual = someone with no sexual drive; solosexual = someone who gets off alone but has no interest in partnered sex acts). No matter how you identify, your sexuality isn't an unimportant afterthought, and I'll address the entire spectrum in this book.

At heart, this book is an "anti-dating book" dating book. It scraps all the worn-out ideas of men being from Mars and women being from Venus, not to mention the backwards concept of "acting like a lady, thinking like a man." It scoffs in the face of pretty much every well-regarded relationship expert on TV or otherwise. (As we all know, the old guard's way of relationshipping hasn't worked out so well: we've got a 60 percent plus rate of cheating and divorce, and 45 percent of today's population is single—the highest rate ever.)

In today's hyperconnected online world, we *need* face-to-face interactions with people—which includes dating and sex. Thanks to the pressures of social media and the Internet, people are lonelier than ever before. This isolation is making us sick; in fact, research has found that it's a bigger health hazard than smoking and can even contribute to early death. For these reasons, we should all be reaching out for *more* connection, love, and physical touch, not less. In my world, nobody's faulted for seeking out more love or sex.

The biggest question all my patients struggle with is "Am I normal?" People come to me miserable and searching, but desperate to feel okay as they are. And why wouldn't they struggle? We live in a world that feeds on social comparison. Entire industries are built on knocking down our self-confidence, especially women's. But it doesn't have to be this way, and the radical transformations I've helped facilitate in my work are similar to the ones I want for you as a reader. Every single one of those transformations occurred because my clients finally reached an understanding that *they're okay as they are*. They don't need to change. They don't need to diet. They don't need to invest in new clothes, hair, personalities, or anything else. They can move through the world, date, and fall in love just as they are right this second.

The only path to intimacy is authenticity and vulnerability: being open and honest about every part of yourself. This is why I'll never tell you to lie, scheme, fake disinterest, or play games to "get" the person you want. That's not love—it's manipulation.

One of the biggest myths I counter in this book is the idea that sex, dating, and relationships are trivial and aren't things that will change your life. Dating and sex are among our most significant areas for growth and self-reflection. They're a tool we can use to help liberate ourselves, both from our own negative self-perceptions and from the systems that hold us hostage psychologically and sexually. That's something I learned firsthand when I shifted gears from standard (and problematic) psychology and became a certified sex therapist.

I was educated in a more traditional, psychological framework, one that was, like most of our culture, incredibly sex-negative. My early clinical work was focused on sex addiction, which I now know is one of the most problematic, pathologizing fields. My teachers and peers believed that any kind of sex outside a relationship was unhealthy and that there was only one right way to have sex or be in a relationship. Anything beyond vanilla, monogamous, husband-and-wife, penetrative sex was considered wrong or unhealthy. They also believed that using porn and masturbating "too much" or at all were signs of sex addiction.

I'd always been an activist, but I still inadvertently transmitted some of that negative messaging to my clients. When I began educating myself in a new model centered on feminism, queer politics, and social justice, my entire personal and professional mission shifted. My clinical work finally felt authentic, meaningful, and like . . . me. With this, my clients' lives changed, too.

Since that pivot in my career, I've had years of clinical experiences that prove that sex and dating are both meaningful and profound, with the potential to trigger major internal transformations.

We are here to break the rules, especially when the current trends are unhealthy and keep most of us feeling disconnected and alone. There is so much power in our sexuality, and when you move your sex life beyond the system and its rules, you become even more powerful. How you fuck, sext, and manage your sexuality is an indication of how empowered and liberated you are; it's also an opportunity to change the world.

This book is not another sexist piece of gender-training propaganda. Instead, it calls out the dangerously flawed concept that men and women are "opposites" who require different sexual or relational skills. This erroneous idea of opposites actually becomes its own problem, setting people up for their current dating- and sex-related obstacles. (Stop reading those other dating books!)

We have to unlearn a lot. We have to unlearn the idea that being different or authentic is not cool, beautiful, or healthy. And in order to do that, we need *real* talk.

If you're confused about where you fall on the gender or sexuality scale, this book is for you. If you haven't had a partner in fifteen years, this book is for you. If you're in an open marriage and looking for new insight on how to deepen your primary connection, this book is for you. You may be grappling with the realities of dating a handful of people at once, or wondering whether you're "not normal" for only getting off on anal, or struggling to find your place on a small suburban campus that doesn't quite grasp the definition of identifiers like gender-fluid, pansexual, or nonbinary. This book is for people who *insist* on pushing themselves when it comes to how they view and experience love and sex.

This book will also challenge what so many of us have unknowingly held to be true when it comes to sex and relationships: that porn is bad, that sex addiction is real, and that heterosexuality and marriage are the automatic gold standard for a happy life. It will force you to unlearn what you've been taught all your life. It will show you how redefining your relationships can help you redefine who you are and who you want to be. It might even make you cry—not from shame, but from relief. Like so many of my clients, you will feel freer, happier, and more confident in yourself, just the way you are *right now*.

ALL THEIR RULES ARE WRONG

I want you to start breaking every rule you've ever been told when it comes to sex and dating. Why? For one, the rules clearly aren't working (you're reading this book for a reason, right?). For another, they're dysfunctional. They're outdated. They're sexist and sex-negative.

But the biggest reason? They keep us feeling disconnected and inferior. If we want to start actually *feeling good* about our sex lives, we need to unlearn nearly everything we've been taught—even as far back as that incredibly awkward sixth grade sex ed class. In *my* sex ed experience, the boys and girls were separated into different rooms while an anxious adult rambled on and on about heterosexuality, penetrative sex, anatomy, and procreation. We need so much more than that, because heterosexual penetrative sex in order to have a child is not why most of us have sex! Sex is a massive part of development and is also about pleasure and fun; we need to be talking to kids about masturbation, porn, the beauty of diverse sexual orientations, and the breadth of the gender spectrum.

SEX POSITIVITY: WHAT IS IT?

Being sex-positive means asking for the type of sex you want proudly, using the correct terminology for your sexual anatomy, and never allowing a partner to shame you for enjoying the type of sex you are aroused by. You aren't "slutty"—you are sexually confident. Healthy, confident people have the sex they want, where they want it, and how often they want it.

Cultures with more nudity and more sexually permissive, sex-positive attitudes have lower rates of sex crimes, violence, and unwanted pregnancies. Modesty is rooted in shame and also helps maintain shame. If nudity freaks you out or makes you feel disempowered, examine why and how. This shame may negatively affect you in other ways, too. But for women who feel beat down by respectability politics (page 10), sexism, body shame, and sex phobia, sex positivity is radical, revolutionary, and much needed liberation.

Most traditional dating advice—especially from so-called experts—is centered on archaic, sexist stereotypes about what "men" and "women" are supposed to do, be, and look like. Men want sex, while women fight it off; men are hypersexual initiators, while women are fragile and coy; men are big, hung, and buff, while women are tiny, toned, and tan (with huge boobs, obviously).

All these stereotypes are bullshit, because gender roles are bullshit! Not only are these ideas often incorrect, but they're outright harmful. And despite what so many "experts" insist, those hetero-sexist and misogynist standards *aren't* based on good science or current psychology. They're pulled from messed-up cultural norms that have been in place since years before we were even born, they harm and limit us all, and they negate the realities of an ever-growing population of people who don't fall neatly into society's little boxes. Sexual and gender fluidity are real, people.

Of course, I didn't wake up woke. I grew up in the same toxic American culture most of us did, and early in my career I used to hand out the "hate yourself" Kool-Aid to clients who struggled with sex issues. It wasn't a conscious decision; it was just what I'd been taught—to pathologize healthy parts of everyday sexuality, to view white, cis hetero, monogamous relationships as not just the norm but the ideal for health. Luckily, everything changed when I found feminism, social justice theories, and queer theory.

I realized that I had broken every definition of sexual and social health as defined by the "experts" yet I was still successful and happy. I was dating all genders, and sometimes having open sexual relationships, despite having been taught that healthy sex takes place exclusively within a committed partnership between a man and a woman. My friends and I masturbated as much as possible—sometimes many times a day!—using porn, yet I'd been taught that this was wrong because it was linked to sex addiction (an abusive, made-up term I'll discuss later).

The truth is you can find your own version of happiness, no matter whose rules you choose to follow (or ignore). When you challenge your thinking about your own sexuality and see the truth about our system's toxic mores, you become more powerful (and, in my view, far more healthy). It's time we all learned to rebel against our culture's most absurd expectations. Below I'll explain how to do just that.

THEIR RULE: don't have sex too soon—and never on the first date.

This one is a holdover from your parents' (and grandparents'!) era. Back in the day, women were discouraged from having lives, minds, and careers of their own. Because they had so little actual power out in the world, they were encouraged to use sex as currency—a ticket to marriage, kids, and a "good" life. They were taught that men would lose interest if they "got the goods" too early. Sadly, that outmoded idea is still being regurgitated, even by prominent experts, authors, therapists, and dating coaches. Hello, it's the twenty-first century! Why are we behaving like it's 1949?

Waiting to sleep with someone simply because it's what society has always insisted was normal and respectable is actually game playing. And it's manipulative and dishonest.

Sex is a critical component of any romantic connection, and if you value your sexuality, you don't have to hide it, stifle it, or "save it for later." There's no cogent *reason* to divide up intimacy into a hierarchy. Lead with your sexuality. Commit to seeing where it takes you, even if this means you get naked on the first date—or within the first hour. And if you want to have sex quickly but you can't quite pull the trigger because you've internalized that fear of "What will people think?"—shut it down. I understand how powerful that fear may feel. But it's entirely culturally created. And that's why nonjudgmental, open-minded friends who don't slut-shame are *essential.* If you don't have any, go find some.

SLUT-SHAMING IN ACTION

Most women have reported being slut-shamed at some point in their lives; it's incredibly common. What does that mean exactly? Slut-shaming is judging or denigrating someone for their sex life, history, or choices. Whether someone tried to cut you down because you flirted with a coworker, had sex with a Tinder date, refused to disclose how many sex partners you had, admitted you were assaulted or harassed, or simply wore a short skirt, slut-shaming is never okay. It's also a bigger problem than simply an individual trying to dictate someone else's sexual mores; it's ingrained in our culture and the puritanical ways that we're trained to see sex. Push yourself to help end slut-shaming—whether this means cutting yourself a break for a hookup you regret, refusing to tell a new partner how many others you've had sex with, or making a personal pact to never gossip about someone's sexual choices. Remember, calling someone a slut says nothing about the other person and everything about you.

MY RULE: have sex early. Sex can be a great lead-in to a real relationship.

I literally laugh out loud when I hear someone say, "I'm waiting to have sex because I want to really get to know this guy." Sex *is* a way of getting to know someone—a tool to learn about how much closeness, intimacy, and affection someone enjoys, and a must if you want a long-term committed relationship. For people who say they're delaying sex, is the act just a meaningless, empty banging of genitals to you? And if that's the case, why do those same people who put off sex later ask for monogamy as a way to keep this soulless, impersonal activity solely between them and their primary partner? See the hypocrisy? It's an example of how confused and afraid so many of us are when it comes to sex.

I'm all about consent and personal agency, and I'd never advise someone to have sex if they didn't actively want to. But if you go out on a date and you're feeling each other, and you can't stop imagining what your date's outfit would look like in a heap beside your bed, be bold. Squash the puritanical bullshit and make a move. No high-quality human would reject you for that, and if they did, you wouldn't be compatible anyway.

In my clinical practice, I've seen couple after couple come into my office frustrated, fighting, and miserable because they made sex a low priority in their relationship. They assumed that their sexual satisfaction could be figured out later, that it would "work itself out" if they loved each other enough. Sadly, that's not always true.

I specifically remember working with two heterosexual couples who delayed—or outright ignored—the sexual component of their relationship. Both women married men with low sex drives, and both women told me, "I cannot imagine going the rest of my life without having a guy grab my ass and tell me he wants to fuck me." Because they shelved that part of themselves when they married these guys, both women ended up frustrated, grieving the heightened sex lives they had when they were single and dating.

CLIENT CASE STUDY

I once worked with a man, "Andy," who felt stymied by his lack of success in love. He worked out religiously, spent a ton of money on clothes, had a nice car, and worked sixty hours a week. He felt like he was a good catch, that he was doing all the right things. The problem was that he was doing all the things he'd been *told* to do; he was focused on conformity, on looking the part, not on authenticity. So over a period of months, I helped him break away from what he'd been socialized to believe would make him a "catch." I told Andy to start doing things he genuinely enjoyed, for example, staying in bed to read for thirty minutes instead of forcing himself to the gym every morning. I also told him to cut back on work and focus more on pleasure. Within a year, his world had dramatically expanded. He started volunteering. He adopted a dog. His life felt richer. And it wasn't until then that he met someone; he was living honestly, which allowed him to find genuine compatibility.

When they're dating, some couples delay sex because they think if they do it too soon, the other person will lose interest. Hey, it's happened to all of us, and it sucks. But if someone *does* stop texting you after you sleep together, that is a sign there was no other level of compatibility or interest beyond sex, and they're revealing important information. If sex is literally a person's only interest in you, you need to know that *now*. If they're into you and there are other levels of chemistry and compatibility, they *will* call or text.

When to have sex depends on how soon you really want to get to know someone. Going for dinner or coffee is a great way to learn about what TV shows someone watches, what their career goals are, and whether or not they want kids. But body esteem (the specific way we feel about our bodies' worth and social desirability), deep affection, and real intimacy are uncovered through touch and sexual exploration. By the way, sexual compatibility is also a hugely important factor if you're considering someone for a long-term monogamous relationship. Please don't think that if you love someone enough or find them hot enough, good sex will just happen—it doesn't.

WHAT IS SEXUAL COMPATIBILITY?

Sexual compatibility is a blend of how often you like to have sex (daily, weekly, monthly), what type of sex (kink, vanilla), how much intimacy you crave during sex (lights on/off, eye contact or no eye contact, naked or covered up, full-body play or lots of rules and limits), and sexual-relational configuration (monogamous, open, poly, swinging). Please don't fall in love or commit to someone until this has all been explored. And notice I didn't say "discussed"—I said "explored," because sex is an activity that needs to be felt, experienced, and embodied. You cannot just talk it out. We are sexual beings, and sex is one of our most important tools for connection, fun, bonding, coping, soothing, and entertainment.

My last three serious relationships were initially intended to be sex-only; we hopped in bed first and asked questions later. But after starting to explore each other sexually, we realized there was something real there and figured, hey, we might as well go to dinner. Those dinners eventually became a relationship. Sex encompasses everything: the biological, the physical, the intellectual. When you're on a coffee date, it's easy to stash your true self away; your dynamism and complexity get lost in superfluous chatter about everyday minutiae. But there's no room for bullshit in bed.

THEIR RULE: dress to impress. Make a killer first impression. Do whatever you have to do: lose weight, dress differently, get plastic surgery.

I call bullshit. Strategizing ways to impress someone is just another game. It diverts the focus from making a true connection to simply getting what you want: validation and approval. If you have to try that hard to make someone like you, the chemistry is off and you're not being authentic.

Sure, the idea of wearing something you feel comfortable in instead of something uncomfortable that you look objectively "hot" in might be kind of scary. But the payoff is immense. Dress "sexy" only if that's how you like to dress; then you're staying true to yourself, and the confidence driving that decision is even more alluring to others.

Culture doesn't tell you to love yourself exactly as you are. Makeover shows and gym and fashion culture all spout off problematic narratives of beauty and worth. Changing your body to make it more "lovable" is not body positivity.

MY RULE: date to be known, not liked.

Your goal in dating—and in life—should always be authenticity: this is the only way to find real compatibility. If you are not dating as yourself, then you are misleading your date, being manipulative, and misusing the dating process: the process of looking for a true match. The goal is to find people who accept you for who you are *right now.* Not for who you pretend to be or how you might be ten pounds down the road or when you finally own a car. If you have to dress differently, talk differently, or dumb yourself down to match with someone, then you're cheating them of the opportunity to truly assess compatibility and to get to know and appreciate the real you.

I want you to date *now!* Not once you've lost weight, bulked up,

gotten Botox, or poured your life savings into a flashy (and unneces-
sary) new car.

WHAT ARE RESPECTABILITY POLITICS?

One of the things my social justice peers and I often discuss
is respectability politics: the idea that you need to *appear*
a specific way—like someone other than yourself—to earn
respect (this way is often based on white, upper-class, cis-
gender norms). Most of us live under the stress of respectability politics, but when you're on a date, you should let go
of false presentations. Pretending to be something you're
not—whether that's acting like you make more money than
you do, or wearing a dress you'd never wear, or acting like
you don't want a relationship—will only bite you in the ass
later.

You have value, no matter how you look. Period. Your worth is
not tied to how sexual you appear, what you're wearing, or how flirty
you are. Stop buying into the myth that you should dress or behave
"respectably" in order to be loved. This is the death of authenticity
and intimacy building. There are people out there who will genuinely
vibe with your radical feminist politics, your fat body, or your queer
mind. Wait for them.

My podcast cohost, Amber Rose, serves as a prime example for
mastering the art of not giving a fuck. She recently caught flak from,
well, pretty much the entire Internet after a photographer spotted her
wearing a hat that said "slut" while hanging out at the beach with her
young son. Apparently this made her look "unrespectable" enough
for people to doubt her parenting skills. Or maybe people were just
terrified of her sexuality and the way she embraced the decision to

live in a sex-positive way. Self-righteous, sex-phobic trolls attacked and shamed her, but she wasn't upset; she knows she still deserves respect, regardless of what she wears. More of us should be living brazenly, without apology, like Amber does.

THEIR RULE: don't be too "available."

Playing hard to get—or never appearing too "available"—is game playing and a way to manipulate someone into chasing you. No self-respecting dater should do it. Not only is it demoralizing, but if it actually works, it means the other person's attachment to you is based on, well, bullshit and manipulation. I want you to find someone who sees and knows the real you.

MY RULE: interested people like signs of interest.

Don't play hard to get! Let people you are interested in know you like them. Healthy people want partners who are confident enough to express their feelings openly. For instance, my older brother, who's very self-aware, calls to give me the scoop whenever he's dating a new woman. And if she happens to put out any semblance of "playing hard to get" vibes, he's done. He wants a woman who's as honest and strongheaded as he is and someone who's not afraid to tell him that she's into him.

There is no "right" speed to date, text, or communicate. It's okay to show signs of interest. How often should you see someone you're dating? As often as you want to. Again, show signs of interest. See the pattern here? Moving fast is authentic if that's the speed at which you want to move. Personally, I enjoy moving fast, because I enjoy close relationships with lots of communication. From the very first date onward, I like to text and hang out with the people I'm into as often as possible. The goal of healthy and authentic dating is honesty, not game playing. If the two of you are not compatible, this needs to be known, and it's helpful for both of you to learn where you're at when it comes to speeds and levels of intimacy.

Dear Dr. Chris,

I've been married to the same person for ten years, and while we're very compatible and most aspects of our life together are great, our sex life is starting to slow down and feel a little boring. It seems like we're just going through the motions; there's not a ton of passion there anymore. I still love her and am attracted to her, so I want to stay together, but I've been thinking about talking to my wife about opening up our marriage. I fear she would get upset, possibly to the point of leaving me. I don't want things to grow so stagnant that I end up tempted to stray or cheat, though. Any advice?

DR. CHRIS: It's okay for someone to ask for nonmonogamy, even after they've committed to long-term partnership or marriage. At any point, you're allowed to request changes to your commitment. First, though, I'd suggest sitting down and talking to your wife about the sexual state of the union. Ask her how she feels about your sex life, whether she's satisfied, whether there's anything she wants that she's not getting. See if there are new activities you can try together that might heat things up for you both: kink, a new kind of porn, even a threesome. You haven't mentioned how much work you've both put in (or not put in) to spice things up. If you've already tried a bunch of new additions to your sexual repertoire and you still feel dissatisfied, go ahead and talk to her about opening up your marriage, but be prepared for different reactions. And if she agrees to try it, make sure to determine—together—some clear boundaries to ensure you're both comfortable and prepared.

Plus, pretending you don't care when you actually *do* only serves to denigrate the importance of relationships. I believe our human connections are everything, and I emphasize this with my clients. It's been scientifically proven that nothing makes us happier and more fulfilled than our interactions with others, so those relationships need to come before everything else: before work, before "self-improvement," before buying the shiny new toys you don't need. Isolation is the most psychologically destructive experience of all.

What if you're inadvertently putting out "hard to get" vibes because you're genuinely not sure how you feel about a person? In that case, I always advocate sticking around a little longer. Text them one more time. Go out with them again.

THEIR RULE: men should make the first move and pay for dinner.

If I have to pay for your dinner in order for you to see me as a "real man," that's good to know. Why? Because it means I no longer want to date you. I know that for some people, there's still dissent over the concept of chivalry, but it's a practice rooted in sexism and misogyny. We need to stop reinforcing the idea that women should expect gendered special treatment and that they should be *actively angry* if a man fails to pay, hold the door, or text and ask them out first.

MY RULE: gender roles are dead. Stop being sexist.

Gender roles have no place in today's dating world. Kindness, yes. Compassion, of course. Respect, always. But chivalry's gender roles are code for sexism, and its history traces back to a time when women were literally treated as property and owned by their husbands. Let's not go back there!

If you are a woman who appreciates traditional gender roles, I don't want to shame you, but I also don't want you to be surprised if this shows up as sexism in other ways, like a guy's demanding sex from you or telling you what to wear in public. If that doesn't sound like fun, reconsider your attachment to having a guy perform false acts of bravado. Take turns paying. Ask him out. Let go of old-school gendered expectations.

THEIR RULE: once a cheater, always a cheater.
This old nugget is often uttered by judgy people who are having a hard time getting past someone's old relationship behaviors—or looking for a reason why someone's previous relationships failed. It implies that some folks can't, won't, and don't have the capacity to change or grow, and it's flat-out wrong. It also puts all the blame on the individual "cheater" instead of on our larger, oppressive relationship system.

MY RULE: monogamy is hard and often doesn't work. Blame the system, not just the individuals involved.
Monogamy has been considered a cultural standard for only about a thousand years. But it's exceptionally hard to have sex with only one person, and the longer we live, the less realistic it gets. Think about it: life expectancy used to be much lower, so we had to be monogamous for only a handful of years. Now many of us are living into our eighties and nineties. The most exciting thing, sexually speaking, is novelty. The more you do something, the more boring it becomes, and monogamy is the opposite of what keeps human beings interested. We don't eat the same meal all the time, or listen to the same song, or watch the same movies, because we'd get bored. Sex is the same way. There's only so much a couple can do to keep it interesting after being together for decades.

Many people can't or don't stay "faithful"—not because they don't love their partners but because having sex with solely one person for the rest of one's life is very, very difficult (I'll touch on alternatives to monogamy in the next chapter).

Exact statistics on how many people cheat are hard to come by because so many people feel ashamed and don't want to fess up to it. Still, recent estimates range from 50 to 70 percent. That doesn't mean that all the people who've strayed are inherently shitty humans who don't deserve to fall in love again. But it does mean that of all the options for ways to deal with their relationship struggles, they chose a damaging one: cheating.

Cheating is hurtful and deceptive, a thoughtless, last-ditch effort to meet one's desire for sexual newness while avoiding a painful divorce or an honest conversation about needed changes. "How will I trust my partner again?" is the common question. You cannot "trust" that you will never be disappointed, upset, uneasy, insecure, or wounded again. You will be. That's an outcome of being in a relationship.

I am not giving someone permission to cheat or condoning cheating. I am saying that monogamy, marriage, and relationships are difficult. If you want to practice monogamy and you're interested in someone who's cheated in the past, try to have a little empathy and compassion and consider the unfortunate truth that many people will cheat *and* get cheated on in their lifetimes. It can be possible to stay together after cheating, as long as the cheater accepts accountability and addresses the issues that led to the damaging behavior.

THEIR RULE: it's "inappropriate" to date someone much older or younger.

Judging someone based on how old they are is rooted in ageism. Instead of limiting yourself to an arbitrary rule about how many years up or down you're willing to go, why not stay open to all possibilities and really see what's out there? You might find yourself surprised.

MY RULE: date you-appropriate people, not age-appropriate people.

Chronological age promises nothing about a person on a deeper level. Psychological age means way more. Also, dating criteria and lists of requirements are all written by our ego: the part of us that keeps us single while saying we want a partnership. These lists are what you *think* you need, not what you actually need, and they stem from a lack of confidence. Age appropriateness, dick size, height, income, weight—all of this is your ego talking, and it keeps you from love by wanting more, bigger, newer, and nicer. Love does not think in these terms, and labels distract us from taking the time to really get to know a person. The minute we label, we lose the authenticity and honesty of who someone is. Categorizing equals stereotypes.

At the end of the day, as a therapist, I still believe in sociology more than psychology. Nothing is individual. Everything is the result of the system or culture you've been embedded in. Let's say I'm forty and I meet a potential partner who's also forty. Everyone might immediately assume he's "age-appropriate." But what if he's been raised in a body-shaming, toxic, hypermasculine culture for forty years? What if he's racist or homophobic or abusive, or he wants utterly different things from life and relationships than I do? Then he's probably not appropriate for me. Now let's say I meet someone who is twenty and a social justice feminist, with values and a lifestyle similar to my own. She may be younger, but what matters is her values and ethics—how relationally healthy she is. She'd obviously be a better partner for me, assuming she's looking for the same kind of relationship I am.

Age promises nothing. Our biological age is not our psychological, spiritual, or sexual age. Date and partner with those you love and are attracted to. Ignore ageist rules and constructs; instead, focus on compatibility and chemistry.

THEIR RULE: don't date too soon after a breakup, and don't date someone who's "rebounding."

People have created all kinds of self-imposed and self-invented rules about how soon is "too soon" when it comes to dating again after a breakup. Some people force themselves to wait a month. Some give themselves twice as long as the relationship lasted to "get over it" (far too long, everyone!). But in my experience, rebounds aren't real.

MY RULE: date someone whenever. (Again: rebounds aren't real.)

I understand someone's hesitation to get involved with a new partner who's just been dumped, but in reality, there's no "correct" amount of time one should take off after a breakup. The length of time between relationships does not determine the health or sustainability of the next relationship. Someone may be hurting a little, but they're not irrevocably damaged after a breakup. In fact, getting back to sex or dating sooner than later can actually help you feel better. In my experience and my clients', the easiest, best way to get over a heartbreak is to get back into sex and dating.

When I get out of a relationship, I'm usually back on dating sites that night. Some people might perceive that as being "too fast," but I enjoy being reminded that I'm desirable and have options. Relationships feel good to me and I prioritize them above everything else.

Plus, the concept of a "rebound" isn't real, kind of like the "having sex too soon" myth. If we have sex on the first date and I find us compatible, I'll be thinking about you and curious about you, and I'll actively want to see you again. The idea of a rebound relationship is the same. If I meet someone really great, I'll be excited and available to them, regardless of whether I just got out of a relationship yesterday or years ago.

STOP IT WITH THE DATING TIMELINES

Most of our lives are just one trauma after another—some of them minor, some of them massive. There's no such thing as "too fucked up" to be in a relationship, and there's no such thing as dating too soon after being heartbroken. For example, let's say I got fired today, and two days later I got offered a great job. Would you tell me to turn the job down because it was "too soon" for an amazing new job? Would you tell me to chill out and recover for a while? "You really should take a couple of months and learn how to be without a job before you go into that new job, because you don't want to bring all the bullshit from that last job into your new job." Nope, no one would say that because it would be ridiculous. Same goes for dating.

CHAPTER 1 WRAP-UP

BE AUTHENTIC; DON'T PLAY GAMES.

HAVE SEX SOONER RATHER THAN LATER.

DATE TO BE KNOWN, NOT TO BE LIKED.

STOP THINKING IN TERMS OF GENDER.

**SEX CAN BE A LEGITIMATE WAY
INTO A RELATIONSHIP.**

**GAME PLAYING IS FOR PEOPLE WHO ARE
UNSURE OF THEIR WORTH.**

**DON'T PLAY HARD TO GET—
INTERESTED PEOPLE LIKE SIGNS OF INTEREST.**

NORMAL IS NOT THE GOAL

When it comes to sex, love, relationships, and personal identity, "normal" should not be the goal. (What does normal really *mean*, anyway?) Sexual and gender identity extends way beyond two-option, straight or gay, male or female checkboxes. There is no one-size-fits-all when it comes to human sexuality. In fact, you're free to reevaluate what it means for you day by day, month by month, or even minute by minute. Despite this, there are sexual and gender-based norms that society sets for us, and living outside these norms is powerful and brave.

This chapter will explore types of sexuality that fall beyond norms. It's not an encyclopedia, so it won't touch on everything; that would be impossible. It's more about giving you space to explore and identify what feels comfortable to you, because fluidity is healthy. You don't need to force yourself to pick any one identity, either; it's okay to embrace the uncertainty of not totally knowing. There are hundreds of terms that fall in between the experiences and identities we're going to talk about here, and they're all legitimate. You get to decide what these terms mean for you and whether they're useful in understanding and embracing your (or your partner's/partners') sexuality.

Whether you came to being heterosexual, trans, asexual, homosexual, or bisexual via biology, choice, early life experiences, or a past relationship, just know that you are healthy, you have worth, and you can and should live your sexuality proudly.

My Story

I didn't always know how to live my own sexuality proudly. I was raised in a traditional two-parent, heteronormative household and attended private Catholic school for years. Though I wasn't raised religious at home, I was shoved into plenty of small, narrow-minded, "traditional" boxes. My parents assumed I was exclusively straight, because there was no other option in their book. They assumed that I'd eventually marry a woman, have a couple of kids. The story—*my* story, not theirs!—only had one conceivable ending.

So I fell in line and acted in accordance with the norm: I played the role of the prototypical young, horny cis hetero dude. I dated and had sex with women, and for most of my teenage years I remained comfortable in that lifestyle; the story had no other ending, remember? But in high school, something shifted. I started hanging out with the edgy, rock 'n' roll misfit kids; you know the ones.

By that point I'd begun realizing I was also into men, and also those who lived beyond traditional genders. My new friends were outspoken, proud, and unrepentant about their sexual choices, and they introduced me to the revolutionary idea that *I didn't have to choose*. Who said I had to be heteronormative? Who said I couldn't date people of all genders, on all sexual spectrums? Once I gave myself permission to explore these desires, my world opened up. As cheesy as it might sound, I was finally able to be free.

Of course, as you can imagine, my newfound openness wasn't warmly embraced by all my friends and family. You see, there's this disturbing belief in mainstream cis hetero culture that if you have sex with a guy *even once*, there's no coming back from it. You're not bi, because in mainstream culture, bi doesn't exist; instead you're straight-up gay. Somehow, heterosexual women who flirt with—or even sleep with—other women are granted some leeway to dabble. Hey, it's cute and harmless! Even women who leave their male partners for women are allowed to return from that. But men are often unfairly given less freedom to explore and are expected to uphold strict standards of masculinity. Those standards are toxic, by the way, hence the buzzword "toxic masculinity."

Men are expected to be strong and stoic, as well as virile and sex obsessed. And for many cis hetero women, if a man has fucked another guy even once, he's automatically seen as gay. Likewise, the gay community doesn't always buy into bisexuality or sexual fluidity. In my high school years I wasn't able to comfortably claim my fluid identity, and was actually forced to walk away from both communities for a while to find my own sense of comfort with who I was. After I began dating in the broader nonnormative queer community (a group of people who might like the opposite gender sometimes but don't want to be held to any rigid expectations about how they'll date, live, have sex, or dress), I finally realized I could identify based on what felt right for me.

TOXIC MASCULINITY: WHAT IS IT?

Toxic masculinity is the cultural reinforcement of tired, oppressive stereotypes linked to manhood: what it means to be a "real man." For instance, the idea that "real" men are aggressive, domineering sex machines who stow their feelings away and remain "strong and silent." These ideas also manifest in the way men are socialized to avoid anything considered "feminine." Cis men are taught to avoid traditionally "girly" pastimes and colors. Think no pink, no cooking, no sewing.

It's important that you know now, if you didn't already, that *you don't have to choose.* Your sexuality, desires, and attractions can and should morph over time. So if I'm with a man, that doesn't mean I identify as gay or that I'm no longer attracted to women. Healthy sexuality lies in fluidity. It is refusing to adhere to rigid rules or expectations about what it means to have a penis or a vagina. It is being open and malleable, allowing multiple possibilities to exist within yourself.

You Don't Have to Choose

I don't believe in official definitions when it comes to sex and identity. If a client comes into my office and says, "I'm gay," I respond, "Tell me what that means to you," because I honestly don't know. Same goes if a client tells me they're straight. Everyone's understanding of their sexuality is different. For instance, someone might tell me something along the lines of "Well, I like women, but every now and then I get a blow job from a guy."

Part of what I try to do is help my patients find their way beyond shaming, limiting diagnostic labels. I've watched so many clients feel relieved when I tell them that they don't have to choose between "gay" or "straight," because so much of the conflict around sexual and gender identity is this false idea that you have to pick a sexuality and identify as one label or the other.

For example, I worked with an actress who confided in me about her childhood: how she'd been raised as a girl and was always told she was a girl, so of course she bought into it, the same way I did when my parents told me I was cis. Still, she never felt completely comfortable in her skin; something just felt off. Then one day she put on a "man's" suit, wore it on the red carpet, and felt this powerful rush of relief as one of the truest sides of herself was finally allowed to emerge. Of course, it wasn't the *only* side of her, and when I told her that her identity was up to her to define, she was blown away. I told her that if she felt unsure but still wanted to identify, she could identify as queer, which means simply not being normative. She told me later that my simple words of encouragement changed her life and shifted her entire perception of sexuality—both her own and other people's.

SEXUAL INTERSECTIONALITY

No one can speak for everyone. Sexual intersectionality means that everyone's sexuality is affected by the privileges and oppressions that are incorporated into their identity. We need to take all those elements into consideration because we don't all have the same choices at our disposal, or the same cultural support, when it comes to exploring our sexuality.

Certain people will be more shamed because of their identities. If you're a woman of color, you're already getting more systemic slut-shaming, so a white woman generally might have more social confidence to explore things sexually, be openly polyamorous, or ignore certain sexual norms.

We can start to notice, in small ways, before getting naked with someone how differences in race, gender, age, and other characteristics factor into how we feel about being emotional, and sexual, and expressing ourselves.

EVERYTHING IS NATURAL

Animals have been comfortable with their sexualities and identities for as long as they've been alive. Consider that there are a lot of animals that change their genders (clown fish and eels) and don't need a partner to give birth (Komodo dragons). There are gay animals (lions and penguins), animals who have sex for fun (bonobos), even animals who masturbate (walrus, elephants, turtles). Nature includes everything. It's not gay or straight, male or female. We're the only species that obsesses about such labels.

Your Life, Your Definitions

I always support my patients in creating new terms and labels to describe their sexuality, gender, and other ways of being, because I think it's incredibly important for building a healthy life. Sex, gender, and relationships suffer when we dump meaningless labels on things that don't need to be defined in "traditional" ways—things that can actually be defined however we want them to.

For example, someone doesn't have to be a friend, a girlfriend/boyfriend, a partner, or a fuck buddy; what about the thousands of variations that exist in between? "Fuck buddy" doesn't honor the depth of the relationship for someone who might crave sex, intimacy, and closeness but does not want monogamy, commitment, or formal dating. Scrambling to fit into just a few outdated options (or fit someone else into those options!) will only upset and frustrate you. It's smarter to create new definitions that expand your language to meet your needs. So instead of adjusting to language, make language adjust to you.

Therapists, friends, and even random people on the street love pathologizing and labeling other people's sexual desires. Making someone pick one label—a label that determines a great deal about your life, how you'll live it, who you'll live it with, and how you'll be treated—and then hold to that label for the rest of their lives is unfair, even cruel. It's not honest, it's not authentic, and you could end up feeling trapped by it. Instead, it's healthier to allow these labels to shift.

Marriage Doesn't Mean Anything

We live in a culture that tells us there's only one way to be a healthy, functioning sexual adult: monogamy and marriage. You find someone, you commit to them, you swear off sex with others, and you blindly pour all your time, money, and self-worth into that relationship. If you're a girl, you're told via Disney movies, kids' books, and Barbie dolls (not to mention parents, teachers, and misguided friends) that being a wife and mom is the most important role you'll ever play. If you're a man, you're told that your career is top priority because you're supposed to "bring home the bacon" and take care of your perfect bride and those imaginary future kids you may or may not actually want.

I'm here to remind you: marriage doesn't mean anything. The standard of cis marriage as the be-all and end-all for human sexuality is destructive. "Maleness" and "femaleness" are made up. Heterosexuality is made up. Marriage is made up. They're all social constructs that don't have value beyond what we've ascribed to them. This doesn't mean that monogamy isn't valid or that marriage doesn't work for some people. What it means is that marriage and monogamy don't work for *all* people. There *are* choices out there, and we need to see those choices reflected in the world around us.

Nearly from birth, most of us aren't shown any other way. Because you're not shown any other way, you start to believe there *is* no other way. The media is guilty of this, too. Though we're finally starting to see occasional depictions of healthy sexuality, the media rarely depicts complicated gay, queer, fluid, or bi characters that feel deep or true to life. We don't see movies or TV shows about married couples who realize they want to open up their relationship for a couple of years, or a wife who decides she wants to be with a woman for a while, or a happy couple who sleep in separate bedrooms or houses.

We don't even see accurate representations of casual dating or sex; instead we see hip but confused twenty- and thirtysomethings treating casual hookups and short-term flings as meaningless stops along the way to marriage. We're rarely shown that casual sex can be meaningful on its own. And we're *never* shown healthy depictions of "alternative" types of nonmonogamy, like polyamory or open marriage.

Not seeing any role models on TV that accurately depict healthy alternative sexualities—or any nonnormative sexuality at all—does us a big disservice, and it causes people to falsely assume that "nontraditional" relationship models don't work. It takes guts to admit that you can't sleep with exclusively one person for the rest of your life and that you require other outlets. Nonmonogamy can be a beautiful thing, but we see no public examples of strong, happy, open relationships because there's still so much stigma attached to it.

No matter how great your relationship is, you simply can't stand in front of someone as an adult and tell them that you know for certain you'll want to be with them forever—because it's not true. You might want to be with them *right now*, and you might strongly believe you'll feel that way forever, but no one can predict the future, and there's a pretty solid chance that how you feel today won't be precisely the same as how you'll feel in twenty years. Humans are constantly changing. Healthy sexuality is about forward motion, fluidity, and admitting that what works for you may look different from what works for everyone else.

Nonmonogamy Is a Many-Splendored Thing

For some people, an appropriate alternative to the rote marriage-and-monogamy track is nonmonogamous relationships. There are various kinds of nonmonogamous relationships out there, from open relationships to polyamory to "relationship anarchy." (Relationship anarchy is a type of nonhierarchical relationship that is totally self-defined.) All of these honor the fact that we can love more than one person at a time, that wanting more intimacy and relationality is a healthy thing, and that not all relationships must include sex or use sex to determine which partners are a priority. Again, when it comes to your love life and what works for you, I encourage you to define what you need on your own terms.

There are plenty of books, websites, and speakers out there focused on the pluses and minuses of nonmonogamy. This book is broader, so I'll leave those details to the others, but I want to emphasize that nonmonogamy *is* a valid choice and there's nothing to feel ashamed about if you decide to try that route. It's perfectly natural to want to have commitment, love, and sexual closeness with more than one person in life. In fact, acknowledging that you need something other than monogamy is a sign of self-awareness and authenticity. It shows that you're committed to honoring yourself and that you're in tune with what's right for you.

The most important thing when dating or maintaining relationships with more than one person at once is that *it needs to be practiced with compassion and consent.* I'll touch more on these issues in Chapter 4, but it's crucial that there are clear boundaries in place when engaging in nonmonogamy. Unless otherwise established with a primary partner, everyone involved must know about the other partners; if that's not happening, the relationship can't be considered 100 percent consensual (more on this later).

Let's now talk about some of the unique varieties of sexual identities, experiences, and forms of arousal. Remember, just because they may be different doesn't make them unhealthy. All the terms used in the next section are open to interpretation; they're not meant to be definitive and they will play out in various ways for various people. If these words don't feel useful in describing your experience, don't use them. I'm providing them only to help illustrate the breadth and depth of sexuality and to help people determine what's true for them. Once you have the language, you can start to explain who you are, what you need, and feel more understood yourself.

CLIENT CASE STUDY

I tell my clients to try to view their current sexuality as a starting point. We are all far kinkier than we realize: sex has no limits other than those we place on it, which are far too uptight.

For some people, *kinky* can be a scary word used to describe sex acts that make us anxious, and maybe even turn us on, but that we might be afraid to own. Kinky sex could be what helps save your sex life and your long-term relationship, and it could also help you learn about yourself. In fact, I became a sex therapist because I learned that the lesser-known and more neglected parts of our sexualities are often what turn us on the most. Discussing your kinks and fantasies is one of the most powerful acts of care and commitment because it's the ultimate sign of wanting true intimacy. It's super-vulnerable.

A client, "Jesse," came in to see me for an individual session once, and they were interested in trying something they thought their partner might be, well, a bit put off by: they wanted to bring someone else into bed with them. (My client was nonbinary and used they/them pronouns.) They hadn't broached the subject with their partner yet, but I told Jesse to be as open and honest as possible, as soon as possible, because one of the most important aspects of a strong relationship is feeling deeply seen and known. Your partner can't love you if they don't truly *know* you, right?

When told about any sexual preference, fantasy, or kink, the partner on the receiving end—and I told my client this—should always say "thank you." Whether they're into it or not, their first comment would ideally be something like "Thanks for caring enough about me that you want to be this close. Thank you for sharing the deepest parts of yourself. It is a compliment that you care that much about us."

Another thing the receiving partner must not do is shame. Even if you're not comfortable with the act your partner is suggesting, don't respond with any kind of comment or sentiment that resembles "ew" or "gross."

And further: don't shut it down immediately! Your options are "no, thank you," "maybe, but with some edits," or "yes, please!" Your partner's request for diverse or colorful sex is your opportunity to explore, expand, and have more fun together.

A trusted partner will take the time to think about whether they might be turned on by a new sexual activity. If you mull it over and realize it's not for you, respond kindly and say something like "Wow, thank you for sharing that with me. That's not something I'm interested in right now," but offer other ideas for things you might like to try instead. A shared sex life is an ongoing negotiation. And honestly, you can't know unless you try, so all couples should use these kinds of conversations as a way to grow and maybe give something new a chance, because we're more sexually creative and fluid than we think we are.

Jesse ended up telling their partner what they wanted, and though their lover was resistant at first, after discussing it a bit more, the couple agreed to try it together.

Asexuality

Someone who is asexual may not feel sexual attraction toward others. Accordingly, they may not feel a drive toward sex with partners at all. They're quite capable of falling in love, however, and may still crave relationships and romantic companionship. Will an asexual person be geared toward masturbation? Sometimes, because they might still feel the urge to get off. And being asexual doesn't mean someone *never* has partnered sex; there are many reasons that asexual people might choose to occasionally engage in sex to help build intimacy or to be closer with a partner. Asexuality doesn't connote sexual repulsion or thinking that sex is "dirty." It's more like sexual neutrality, being able to take sex or leave it.

I once worked with a beautiful young couple who were full of energy, so of course an average person would look at them and assume, "Oh, they're obviously fucking a lot." But in reality, the woman complained that her husband rarely wanted sex. She said he seemed "uninterested" in it and she tossed this out in an accusatory, shaming way, as if it meant he wasn't "manly" or sexually healthy. She had even taken him to doctors to test his testosterone levels (they were fine). I told her the truth: she was gendering their relationship struggles and applying values born out of toxic masculinity. Just because someone identifies as a man doesn't mean he's inherently hypersexual, or even sexual at all! I asked her to consider the idea that her partner might be asexual. While she was alarmed at first, he was quite comforted by the idea of asexuality; it helped him realize he wasn't broken.

We worked together on helping the wife mourn the loss of the sex life she'd assumed she'd have, and I helped them explore other ways to be sexual and relax when it did happen. Of course, in a case like theirs, it's also possible that the couple simply isn't sexually compatible—this can and does happen, too, and is unfortunate. If there's a fundamental lack of sexual common ground between you and your partner and it feels like you're just not on the same page, sometimes separating and finding a more sexually suited partner is your best bet.

BUT WHERE DO I GO TO FIND PEOPLE WHO ARE INTO THE SAME STUFF I AM?

Let's say you're into some sexual practices that don't meet the standard cis hetero norm. If you're not sure where to go to find like-minded people to date or hang out with, here's my suggestion: go online. If you skip out on dating websites, you'll be relegated to the usual real-world suspects: the bar, the supermarket, or (if you're lucky) friends of friends. Dating sites automatically provide more options. There are more people on these sites, and with more people comes more likelihood that you'll find what you're looking for. You'll also have the space to decide exactly how to describe yourself, so you can present a full, accurate picture of who you are and what you're into. Some of these sites now have around thirty options when it comes to gender and sexual choices. That's why I love online dating: you can write, "I'm poly," "I'm queer," "I'm asexual," "I don't identify." Your candor in showing who you really are helps pave the way for others to feel comfortable doing the same, and more important, you'll be more likely to find a partner you're looking for.

Aromanticism

The way an asexual person feels about sex can be likened to how an aromantic person feels about love and relationships. An aromantic could have a smorgasbord of sexual partners and could experience deep and emotional feelings of love, but without ever being interested in a deeper romantic relationship. In fact, aromantics often derive happiness, pleasure, and nonromantic love from their platonic friendships, family relationships, and sexual liaisons. Some might also have a primary relationship, which is typically a platonic partnership or deep friendship.

We used to shame asexual people, claiming they had some kind of hormonal issue. We used to shame aromantic people, too, saying they had an intimacy disorder. Nope, no intimacy disorder here. Just like asexuals, aromantics aren't defective or in need of "fixing." It's just a different way of being.

Demisexuality

Demisexual people need to feel strongly invested in someone before they experience sexual desire or attraction toward them. It doesn't necessarily mean they're disinterested in sex; they're not asexual— they just need an emotional bond before they feel comfortable having a sexual relationship. This can sometimes be confused with erotophobia (fear of sex) and sexist ideas about how the female gender should operate sexually. Our culture is so anxious about sexuality that many struggle to understand their authentic sexual arousal template. As you unload your own culturally driven baggage, you will begin to see that your sexuality is far more expansive than you knew.

Solosexuality

A solosexual is someone who's geared primarily toward masturbation or sex with themselves. This type of sexual orientation is often misunderstood, and it's something I see often when clients come in to my office complaining about a partner who "masturbates all the time." Again, this behavior might not mean that the partner is hypersexual or disinterested in the relationship; it might just mean that they're solosexual.

Now that we have language to describe these sexualities, I want single men and women to feel able to be up-front about their sexuality when they're dating, so they can confidently say they are more geared toward this or that. Perhaps they like having a partner and enjoy having sex with them sometimes, but most of their sex life is geared toward sex with themselves, as in the case of a solosexual. So, they might not be the right partner for someone if they want a lot of partnered sex. Different sexualities might make sense for different partnerships.

Kink: We All Fall on the Fetish Spectrum

You can be aroused by anything, and that's okay. If you've thought of it, there's a community of people out there who are turned on by it. Sometimes you'll find yourself more turned on by body parts, clothing items, or particular situations than you are by a person. That's healthy and awesome. When it comes to sex, in fact, *most* things are healthy and awesome. If it's consensual and compassionate, it's not off-limits.

Fetish sexuality is one of the most pathologized and stigmatized forms of sexual expression out there. Practices like BDSM (bondage, dominance, sadism, masochism) and exhibitionism, group sex, and foot fetishes are often described as "edgy" or "fringe" simply because they fall outside the lines of vanilla penis-in-vagina sex. The thing is, we *all* fall somewhere on the kink continuum. In fact, tons of people incorporate elements of kink in their sex lives without realizing it; kink doesn't have to mean BDSM, leather, whips, or chains.

Asking your partner to slap your ass or pull your hair while having sex is low-level BDSM. Telling your girlfriend you'd like her to wear a leather skirt or high heels in bed has kinky elements. There are people out there who might not be exclusively into feet, but they do enjoy massaging, looking at, or sucking a partner's toes from time to time. That's why I prefer to use the word *kink* instead of *fetish—fetish* has a tinge of judgment and is often misunderstood.

In my practice, I encourage my clients to engage in new and different kinks to help them gain confidence and stave off sexual boredom. Trying new things is healthy and you don't necessarily know what will turn you on, or who you fully *are*, until you've explored a variety of types of sex. When my clients come in, I'll ask, "What turns you on?" If someone responds, "Sex with hot women," I'll tell them that's not defined enough. "Yeah, but not *all* women," I'll say. "Come on, what specifically?" Then they'll start breaking it down and realizing their attraction hinges on specific types, scenarios, and body parts. Maybe the woman is wearing something special; maybe she's saying something special. In a similar vein, when I ask my clients about the porn they watch, it's intended to be a powerful way of understanding their core erotic arousal template. I'll ask them, "What are they doing in the video? What scene did you orgasm at? Were they saying something particular? Wearing something? What were their body types?"

This is all about fetishizing. Sex is never just sex. It's deeper and more complicated than we give it credit for.

Dear Dr. Chris,

I started dating a friend of a friend a few months ago. Things were going great and our sex life was fine at first. But recently he started suggesting that I do things I'm not comfortable with. Like he wanted me to wear a leash and a dog collar during sex. I agreed to try it; why not? After that, he asked me to pretend to be a dog and eat and drink from bowls on the floor. I resisted that request, but when we talked about it more, I learned that his ideal relationship would be a master-slave one in which I'm always subservient to him. I don't mind a bit of power play in the bedroom, but I have no interest in being a full-time sub. Should I break it off?

DR. CHRIS: In all relationships, you'll experience moments of disconnect and imperfection. It's rare that you'll meet someone whose sexuality is completely compatible with yours—someone who wants the same kind of sex you do, the same amount of times, in exactly the same way. That's just rarely how life goes. Relationships are about learning how to maneuver and work with that frustration and disappointment. But there's no right way to be sexual, so you can't be mad at someone, or shame them, or demand they change. It's about understanding who your partner is sexually, having a conversation about it, and figuring out what you want to do together as a couple. If you can't find common ground, perhaps it's time to move along.

People with a partner-centric, heterocentric perspective often call in to my podcast saying, "That has to be wrong—I have a right to be pissed that they're more interested in my feet than my vagina," or "They're more interested in masturbating than they are in having sex with me." But, no. They're not bad or wrong for what turns them on. Sure, be frustrated—but don't be *angry*. That's who they are, and you're learning about who they are. If it's not for you, that's fine.

This is partly why I suggest having sex with a new partner sooner than later. Having sex as an early part of dating will help you establish whether you're sexually compatible. Because whoever you think you are sexually, you're not *just that*. You're more. Every time you're with a different partner, you're a different person, sexually speaking. They each bring out or connect to a different part of you. You might have sex twice a day with one partner, and then you get with someone else and you're having sex only once or twice a week. You might be having a different kind of sex—rougher or gentler—than before, or your partner might have a different body type, or they might be introducing you to acts you've never tried. It's almost like you get to be a virgin again with every new person you fuck.

When It Comes to Arousal, Is Anything Off-Limits?

As a sex-positive feminist therapist and social justice activist, I'm focused on ending oppression, especially regarding sexuality—but I'm *not* a police officer. When it comes to sex, I generally believe that anything legal, consensual, and done between adults shouldn't be off-limits. That said, if you're not comfortable with something a partner is encouraging you to do, it's well within your right to step back and refuse. Don't let yourself get bullied into doing something that doesn't feel right. Because compassion matters here, too. People need to be aware of exactly what they're in for when they agree to a new sexual experience, whether that's being blindfolded and handcuffed by someone they just met or going to a sex club with a partner of twenty years.

We are all human beings and we all deserve basic human respect. If someone says they're fully aware of the risks and gives you their full informed consent to hang them upside down from a hook and smack them in the face, it's your job to respect the trust they've put in you. It's on you to take care of them while you're indulging your fantasies. If you're both on the same page and you've both explicitly stated that much, well, have at it.

That said, there are some very extreme practices out there, and while I don't judge them, I also wouldn't necessarily advise them. I don't personally feel sex should be physically risky or life-threatening. I'd be uncomfortable if a client told me they wanted to do certain things that I thought could put their life in danger, but I wouldn't judge them or label them mentally unhealthy; it's not my place. Plus, people do life-threatening stuff all the time: they ride motorcycles; they jump out of airplanes. I don't skydive because I don't think it's safe.

People in the kink community use the term RACK, which stands for "risk-aware consensual kink." If you're going to engage in activities with risks, it's on you to be aware, do your homework, and engage in it with a partner who knows what they're doing.

Remember, there's no "normal" when it comes to sex and love. Anything can and should be on the table, as long as you and your partner(s) feel comfortable with it and have consented to it. Don't let the hypertraditional masses shame you into feeling like your "different" sexual lifestyle is any less legit than the marriage-and-monogamy track, because it's not. It's more than possible to have a huge, happy, healthy sex life with any type of kink, preference, or orientation on the map—you just have to stay honest and look for the people who "get" you.

CHAPTER 2 WRAP-UP

DIFFERENT IS NOT DISORDERED.

NORMAL IS NOT THE GOAL.

YOU HAVE VALUE, NO MATTER WHO YOU ARE OR WHAT YOU'RE INTO.

WHEN IT COMES TO GENDER, YOU DON'T HAVE TO CHOOSE.

NONMONOGAMY IS GREAT AND VALID.

EVERYTHING IS NATURAL.

WE ALL FALL SOMEWHERE ON THE KINK SPECTRUM.

HAVE SEX NOW!

One of the reasons I like working as a sex therapist so much is that sex is one of the few subjects that still generates an enormous amount of insecurity, anxiety, and fear. Think about it: if you're cool with walking through a grocery store talking loudly on your cell phone about your health woes, your family, or your work drama, yet for some reason you drop your voice, start whispering, or stop talking entirely when it comes to discussing your sex life, can you explain why? For years we've been socialized to believe that recreational sex is somehow "dirty" and to adopt modesty that's rooted in shame, but exactly what makes talking about sex taboo? Sex is everywhere and a bigger part of our lives than we might realize.

This chapter explores why having sex—as much or as little as you want, with whom you want, when you want—is something to be celebrated, not feared or repressed. I'll also explain some of the hurdles and misconceptions that get in the way of having a rich, authentic, self-directed sex life.

We learn about ourselves and our sexuality by *being sexual*, not just by talking about it. It's in the course of these explorations that we realize who we are and what we want most intimately. For example, not all heterosexual guys are "tops." Many men come into my office feeling as though they should be dominant, assertive, or the sexual initiator. But I'll explain to them that they might actually be "bottoms," and that's totally cool, too! This just means they're more submissive, prefer having sex initiated for them, or enjoy more assertive female sex partners. This is definitely a role reversal for some traditional hetero-sexual relationships. But there shouldn't be any judgment attached to it; it's simply good information for someone to have about themselves.

The Myth of the "Opposite Sex"

Most parents also teach kids that there are two "opposing," contra-dictory sexes, male and female, and that when it comes to the way men and women think, feel, and behave, it's guys on one side and girls on the other. *Girls play with this toy; boys play with that toy.* This line of thinking encourages kids to believe that boys and girls are essentially opposite—yin and yang, black and white—and that they think, feel, and love differently. This creates a culture in which it's assumed that men and women fundamentally can't understand each other and that they need to strategize and even manipulate to get what they want or understand each other in the first place. That's sexism, plain and simple. Plus, because boys are taught to avoid anything feminine, they learn to equate being masculine with being superior (hence women are seen as lesser, or as objects).

I roll my eyes every time I hear an expert discuss how "all" women or men think, date, or fuck. The moment someone starts discussing "men" versus "women" I know they actually know nothing about gen-der or sexuality, and books in this vein about what "all women want" reinforce the false narrative that there's only one way to be a man and one way to be a woman.

This idea of two opposite sexes sets both feminism and healthy sex and dating back decades, not to mention killing the concepts of authenticity, honest communication, and self-acceptance. Also, not all women have a vagina, and not all men have a penis. Some have the opposite; some have both. Some men can get pregnant and have their period. Trans and intersex people not only *exist* but also date, fuck, and fall in love (in fact, they're as common as redheads). They're worthy of love and sex, too, and we have to stop othering them.

Training kids to adhere to traditional gender codes can also lead them to mistakenly believe that one gender—male, obviously—is inherently stronger, smarter, or better, simply because it's been given more cultural and institutional power. This can lead to the reinforcement of maleness at all costs; the man's perspective is continually prioritized, and a culture of misogyny and mansplaining develops. In this culture, not trusting women, not believing women, and not acknowledging women's humanity become the norm. Many women, for their part, start to internalize the "male gaze," or their perceived sexual worth in a man's eyes, which can prevent them from feeling ownership over their bodies or sexualities.

Rape Culture

One of the biggest hurdles we all face when it comes to having a healthy relationship with sex is the fact that everything we do, say, and believe is colored by the environment we live in: a rape culture. You've probably heard this term before, and you probably understand it, at least somewhat. But I want to clearly explain its impact for anyone who might not fully grasp how rampant and powerful it is, and how fiercely it plays into so many pieces of the sex and love puzzle.

Living in a rape culture means we normalize certain forms of sexual violence: from catcalling and street harassment to rape, assault, and slut-shaming. We normalize these behaviors early by raising kids in households that promote toxic masculinity (see page 23), encouraging the idea that men need to be tough, hypersexual go-getters who maintain dominance over women and avoid anything feminine at all costs. This sets boys up for problematic views of women as objects: women are seen as sexual tools that are available to men without needing consent.

Rape, harassment, and assault are not just "women's issues"—they're men's issues, too, because men are by far the most frequent perpetrators of these types of affronts. Finding a solution shouldn't fall on women, and women shouldn't be pressured to just "suck it up" and live with it. Instead, men must educate themselves and vow to do better.

Gender Norms Are Sexist and Toxic

Sexism thrives on the idea that men and women are different enough to warrant different treatment. This manifests in all kinds of ways, not just in unequal pay or fucked-up beauty standards. It also appears in accepted cultural norms that might appear, on the surface, to be simple, unloaded gestures. But if a gesture is something that a man wouldn't do for a fellow guy, he shouldn't do it for a fellow woman. The people who are really invested in ideas of chivalry also tend to go deeper with their sexism; they're the ones who end up believing in rules like "don't talk back" or "you're weaker than me, which is why I paid for your dinner and held the door for you." Folks who are rooted in traditional gender norms are rooted in oppressive old ideas, so do not be shocked when they want women at home and pregnant, not working, not talking to guy friends, or not "allowed" to wear makeup out of the house.

Rape culture plays out in our dating lives whenever we start universalizing those supposedly standard male or female behaviors: "he should pay for dinner"; "she should clean up after the meal"; "he should initiate sex"; "she shouldn't mention wanting a long-term relationship if she wants to catch a man." These gendered expectations aren't just antiquated; they actively contribute to a toxic culture that, again, prioritizes the male experience over the female experience and trains men to behave in inappropriate ways. It's on us to stop reading books, listening to music, and supporting artists who normalize these ideas. Don't drag sexist expectations into your love life and then punish people for not living up to them! Dating, fucking, and living outside gender norms will make your relationships safer and hotter for everyone involved.

Sex Positivity: The Crux of a Healthy Sex Life

One way to rebel against all these gendered sex and dating rules—and to start living your absolute hottest sex life ever—is to master the art of being truly sex-positive. Being sex-positive doesn't mean you're climbing inside the pants of everyone who looks at you twice (but if you are, that's cool, too). It doesn't mean saying yes *every single time* someone asks you out. It obviously doesn't mean doing anything you aren't genuinely comfortable with. All it means is that you're sexually authentic and you support the same in others. You embrace your own wants, needs, and turn-ons—the *genuine* ones, not the ones you're told you're supposed to have.

Being sex-positive means not creating false narratives or harsh judgments about what "normal" or "healthy" sex looks like, for you or for anyone else. You can have sex with a different partner five nights a week and be sex-positive. You can also abstain from sex for five years and be sex-positive. It's about your wants and needs.

For example, aside from toxic fitness-culture values, I think the gym is a great place. But there are some weeks when I may not be feeling great or I need to focus on other things, so I choose not to work out. Skipping out on exercise for a week or two doesn't mean I detest the gym, fear the gym, or want nothing to do with the gym ever again. It just means I have other priorities at the moment. It's about your attitude: the acceptance of the reality that having compassionate, consensual sex, when and how you want it, is a healthy, natural thing. Again, there's no "normal" when it comes to sex, so it does not mean you're abnormal or sex-negative if your desires are more solo or kink oriented.

WHAT'S SEX NEGATIVITY?

You can have a lot of sex but still be sex-negative. If you're out there having sex but you're judging yourself (or others) for it, or thinking that you're not a good person because you had a one-night stand, or tried anal sex, or had a three-some, or are having an exclusively sexual relationship with someone, you're exhibiting sex negativity.

My definition of sex positivity also correlates to the idea that we should dismiss the norms that marriage and monogamy are "higher" forms of relationships than casual ones and that waiting to have sex means you are more serious about getting to know someone. There are tons of fucked-up cultural norms out there, but you don't need to drag those into your sex life. In fact, your sex life is one of the only places where you can be truly free from the rules and boundaries of everyday life. Sex positivity is about breaking norms and living in your own sexual authenticity. Being sex-positive means being nonjudgmental about your sex and relationship choices—as well as others'.

Slut-Shaming = Sexual Self-Loathing
One massive form of sex negativity that manifests often, in both our culture and our personal relationships, is slut-shaming. Making someone feel dirty or "less than" because of the number of partners they've had or the type of sex they've chosen to engage in isn't just cruel—it's psychologically abusive and incredibly stigmatizing. It isolates and dehumanizes people instead of acknowledging the depth of their sexualities. Not everyone will have sex the exact same way you do. Some people like more sex, or less sex, with more partners, or with fewer partners. That's okay.

But it's not okay to label, attack, or shame people for those choices, to tear them down and essentially say, "I'm going to use your sexuality against you." Just because you're uncomfortable with someone else's decisions doesn't mean they're wrong; it's on you to look at why you're uncomfortable, not to criticize them for living confidently and going after the kind of life they want. Living loudly, creatively, and confidently is a good thing, and it shouldn't be tamped down or reined in to make others feel less uncomfortable.

Most "sluts" are actually just sexually confident. This is a great thing! We could all use more sluttiness—er, sexual confidence—in our lives. A few suggestions on how to boost your own:

- **HAVE MORE SEX.** Do this with people you're attracted to (obviously!) but also think outside your traditional boxes. Are you interested in that barista from the coffee shop who just happens to be a man, even though you usually date women? Ask him out! See what happens. Life's short.
- **TAKE RISKS.** Your life won't change unless you change it. Ask people out. Give out your number. Chat strangers up. Go to dinners, bars, and parties alone. Try a new kind of sex with someone you wouldn't normally date. Think beyond your typical mold and do things that may not be immediately comfortable—it will be enriching.
- **BE HONEST, AUTHENTIC, AND VULNERABLE IN YOUR COMMUNICATION WITH OTHERS.** Tell people how you really feel and what you really want. If you want a one-night stand, say that. If you're hankering for a lifelong relationship, say that, too. People can't read your mind. The more in touch you are with your own wants—and the more adept you are at clearly verbalizing them—the happier you'll be.
- **MASTURBATE MORE.** Learn what you like in bed. Get really good at getting yourself off. If you can't do this, it'll be hard for anyone else to do it.

HOW TO BE MORE SEX-POSITIVE

- **WATCH YOUR LANGUAGE.** The way you talk about sex is either going to help you heal your sexual hang-ups and make you more sex-positive or do the exact opposite. If you drop the tone of your voice, fail to use the correct words, or fail to speak confidently when you talk about sex, you are reinforcing the idea that sex is shameful. Language is the most powerful tool we have in our culture. We have the power to either shame or heal people—including ourselves—with our words.

- **REFINE YOUR INFLUENCES.** It's important to focus on having healthy people around if you want to be healthy yourself. How do your friends discuss sex? If your friends make off-color or rude remarks, you can set a boundary with them. Do you need to move away from them a bit and find a new crew, or do you need to decide that, as a group, you're going to be more sex-positive, more feminist, and less slut-shaming? By the way, the things you're reading and the music you're listening to also need to be a sex-positive resource. If not, you'll never be able to fully internalize healthy messages about sex.

- **SHOW YOUR BODY.** Your relationship with your body needs to be comfortable and confident if you ever intend to be sexually confident with someone else. Are you hiding your body? Or are you comfortable letting it be seen? I wear short-sleeved shirts that show off my physique and my tattoos. I'm not willing to hide to make other people comfortable.

- **HAVE THE RIGHT KIND OF SEX.** We've already established there's no "normal" when it comes to sex. But if you want to be sex-positive and have a better life overall, you need to walk the authentic, sex-pos walk in your own bedroom. That's why

I always tell my partners what I want sexually. I'm willing to make both of us a little anxious, and I'm willing to be confident and risk having them think I'm slutty. You have to set boundaries, ask for, and prioritize your own desires.

- **INVEST IN YOUR SEXUALITY.** Body-positive pornography, which I'll explain in more detail later on, is a part of my life. I spend money on it because it makes my life richer and happier—engaging in that, as well as buying sex products and toys, proves that it's of value to me. Sex has worth; it's a priority in my life. A lot of men don't own sex products because they don't truly prioritize their own sexuality; often they want to get off quickly. But if you go to a sex store and spend your hard-earned cash on sex toys, you're saying, "This is important to me." And if you're willing to use a toy, that's a sign that you're willing to take time with something—it's kind of like spending the money on cooking a really nice meal at home versus ordering in.

- **PRIORITIZE YOUR PLEASURE.** Are you investing in your sexual growth? Are you going to sex boutiques, watching porn, and buying new goodies to try out? Are you taking time out of your day to engage yourself sexually? If the answer is no, why not? Take a couple of hours to center your sexuality: turn off your phone, take a bath, light some candles, play some music, and spend a couple of hours doing literally whatever makes you feel good. Don't just head to the shower when your roommate or partner's away for a quickie orgasm. Make a production out of it like you would with other forms of self-care. This is a sign you deeply value it.

WHY IS *SLUT* A BAD WORD?

Hurling the word *slut* at someone is considered a nasty insult—especially when it's directed against women—because it's used as a way to control their sexuality: "Don't do anything slutty." "Keep your daughter off the pole." "That dress makes you look like a hooker." Have you ever thought about *why* those things are considered so bad, though? Reality check: it's okay to dress however you like. Your clothing doesn't have to indicate anything about your sexual availability. It's no one's place to say what is or isn't appropriate when it comes to sex or attire.

Bad Sex

Anyone who's had sex knows that it doesn't always go the way you expect or desire. When two people get naked together, each person is bringing their own special blend of issues, fears, and boundaries to the table. But being sex-positive is also about accepting that sometimes you'll have disappointing or "meh" sexual experiences, no matter how open, welcoming, and sexually healthy you are. Being sex-positive is about honoring the full range of experiences that can come along with sex: sometimes it's good; sometimes it's bad; sometimes it's mediocre, uncomfortable, or difficult.

It's kind of like going to the movies. Who hasn't walked into a movie really excited, expecting something amazing, then walked out saying, "Oops. That's completely not what I thought it would be"? But that doesn't mean you'll refuse to ever see another movie for as long as you live. In the same way, having less than stellar sex doesn't mean it's time to swear off sex entirely. Just step back if you need to; taking breaks is fine.

Dear Dr. Chris,

I'm a nineteen-year-old woman who became sexually active last year when I went to college. Since then, I've been having a lot of fun hooking up with different people, learning what I like and don't like. I don't have any regrets about my sexual behaviors; I'm just having a good time. My friend always guilt-trips me about it, though, saying I'm insecure and using meaningless one-night stands as a way to get "validation." Is she right?

DR. CHRIS: In a nutshell: nope, she's wrong. In my world, there are no "bad" or unjustified reasons to have sex. Sex can be had for a multitude of reasons, or for no reason at all! You can be looking for fun, love, entertainment, experimentation, physical touch, comfort, orgasm, procreation, or a way to ease boredom. If you feel good about the sex, do it. If it's compassionate and consensual, do it. (Of course, this means you and your partner should both be sober enough to say yes to everything that's happening.)

If you want to use sex for validation, have at it! We should all be deriving more of our sense of validation from our relationships with others in our lives, because humans are relational. Our self-esteem is built on the relationships we're in, including the sexual ones; even the one-night stands and casual hookups. People reflect our worth back to us. Use that to your advantage. Be around people who reflect good things; don't be around people who are toxic or put you down. It's okay to have sex to feel good. Don't buy into the way your friend is framing it—she's projecting her own sex negativity onto you.

YOU'RE A SLUT-SHAMER IF . . .

You criticize someone's outfit for being too tight, too short, or (fill in the blank here).

You mock someone's sexual preferences, kinks, or desires for being "weird" or out-there.

You freak out when a new partner tells you the number of people they've had sex with.

You tell your friends not to have sex on the first date.

You interrogate your nonmonogamous friends about why they don't want a "real," committed relationship.

You shush people when they're talking about their sex lives in public.

You have different standards for how women and men should behave in the bedroom.

You judge how fast other people choose to jump in or out of relationships.

In a Perfect World, We'd All Be Sexually Open

In a perfect world where sexism and toxic masculinity didn't exist, people could appropriately hit on and ask out whomever they found attractive or interesting. Guys could try giving or receiving oral sex to other guys to see what it's like and not get labeled. In a perfect world, I'd encourage everyone to have sex with people of every gender just to try it—because openness is healthy, and pushing yourself is good for you, and you don't know what you're into until you try. Think back to your early sexual experiences: what arouses you has changed and expanded to include new behaviors, experiences, and types of partners over time. Your sexuality is plastic and it has the ability to consistently change and evolve throughout your life.

Few people are exclusively hetero. Recent studies show that as many as 56 percent of millennials don't define themselves as hetero;

they are healthy enough to identify as bisexual, fluid, gay, nonidentified, or queer—or better yet, hetero while allowing for same-sex encounters if and when they want. I tell my patients and my podcast callers to not identify as anything when it comes to sex. Stay open to all possibilities, allow yourself to be surprised, and stay radical.

That said, most of us need to work on sex positivity *first*. If we're still carrying a ton of internalized shame and baggage, learning about yourself sexually just won't be as much fun.

No Sex Is "Safe"

Protecting yourself is about *safer* sex and what level of risk feels okay for you. Just the thought of contracting an STD can trigger sexual panic for some people and actually lead them toward sexual anorexia (denying themselves of any sex at all). That's not what we want. Sexual health is about your sexual attitude and comfort as well as sexual responsibility. Remember, *you* are the person who is most responsible for your sexual health.

When it comes to safer sex, it's on *you* to:

- Ask your partner when they were last tested.
- Get tested. Everyone who is sexually active should be doing this regularly, regardless of anatomy, gender expression, or age. Getting tested is an act of self-care *and* compassion for your partner(s). Remember, healthy sex always takes into account its impact on other people—their physical health included.
- Disclose to partners and prior partners any STDs you currently have (or believe you might have). This is ethical sex. If someone calls you to tell you that they tested positive and that you should get tested, say "thank you," because their call was most likely difficult and was done as an act of care for you.
- Remember that certain STD tests address certain things.

You'll probably need a urine test *and* a blood test if you want to get an extensive picture including HIV, herpes, chlamydia, syphilis, and gonorrhea. In short: make sure you proactively *ask your doctor* to test for everything; don't just assume they will.

- Being sexually careful isn't just about STDs; it's also about the impact of other sex-related health factors. For example, the vagina has a sensitive balance of bacteria and anal sex can lead to microtears. Use lube to help you and your partner be comfortable and help prevent anal and vaginal tearing.

HIV Prevention

Condoms are great, but there are other ways to help reduce your risk of contracting or transmitting HIV:

- PrEP (pre-exposure prophylaxis) is a pill that helps prevent HIV-negative people from being infected with the virus. It reduces risk of HIV contraction more than condoms do, and it's available for use by people of all genders and sexual orientations. Ask your doctor or local health clinic about it if you want to learn more.
- TasP (treatment as prevention) refers to HIV prevention methods that use antiretroviral therapy medication (ARVs) to decrease someone's risk of HIV transmission. TasP involves prescribing antiretrovirals to people who are living with HIV in order to minimize the amount of HIV in their blood to undetectable levels. This means there is effectively no risk of transmission of HIV.

STDs and Shame

No sex is totally safe, but lots of people still feel somehow "dirty" if they contract an infection from sex. Having an STD doesn't make you less "clean" than anyone else; it simply puts you in the company of many. One in two sexually active people will contract a sexually transmitted infection by age twenty-five. These conditions are incredibly common and having an STD doesn't make you icky, wrong, or bad. You can still have a hot, fulfilling love life while also having an STD—even a lifelong one.

If you are sexually active and you and your partner(s) haven't been tested, you have a high risk of getting an STD. Contracting an STD is no different from getting the flu from someone on the bus or a cold sore from a relative's peck (which is actually where a lot of herpes comes from). Treating an STD any differently from how you'd treat the flu is sex-negative. If you can tell your friends that you have been home popping zinc and blowing your nose, why is it shameful to tell them, "My penis burns when I pee because I had sex last night"?

If you're grappling with how to talk to a new partner about the fact that you have an STD, I'm not going to tell you exactly what to say to make it easier, because let's be real: it probably *won't* be easy no matter how you do it. Regardless, you need to tell them. It might be scary, but that's okay. It's one of those awkward, uncomfortable things that go along with being an adult; sometimes we're forced to have discussions we don't want to have. Sometimes we have to break up with people; sometimes we have to disappoint people; sometimes we have to do shit we don't know how to do. There's no magic potion to ease your anxiety or reduce the chance that the other person might have strong feelings about what you tell them. *You just have to say it.* It's also part of consent. Should you feel embarrassed about it? Nope—again, STDs are incredibly common.

Before someone discloses their STD status, it's important for them to do the work of getting confident with it and conquering any fears, concerns, and lingering sense of stigma about it. You might need to be single for a while as you do this work. I don't want you to feel any shame about having an STD; I also don't want you to *be* shamed by the person you're disclosing your status to.

Sex as Medicine

Very few people truly understand how transformative sex can be. I help people use sex as a therapeutic tool, prescribing various types of sex as "homework" to my patients to help them create a more authentic existence, both in their own sexuality and within their relationships. I tell them: "Use sexual language out in the world. Masturbate. Watch porn. Allow yourself to have sex, even if you're not looking to be in a relationship (and especially if you are!). Go out there and get it on—that's the way to do this homework. If you can accept your sexuality, you can accept more of the other parts of yourself." Here are some of the areas where sex and therapy become entwined in my practice.

Sex for Body Esteem

If you can allow someone to focus on you sexually, and allow yourself to be seen naked and vulnerable in a state of arousal, you're working on your body esteem and intimacy building. Being naked in front of someone is a huge act of pushing through shame, because body shame is maintained through both physical distance *and* sexual avoidance. Exposing yourself and forcing yourself to be seen in the most vulnerable sexual light inherently helps you break free of some of those body fears. Another way to use sex as a tool for your own body esteem is to let someone pleasure you exactly the way you like it. Tell them in clear, direct language exactly what you like and what arouses you. Get comfortable hearing yourself use those words, and own those physical parts of yourself.

Masturbation

You don't need a partner to have amazing sex. I tell most of my clients to masturbate more frequently because there are literally no downsides to it. (And no, there's no such thing as being addicted to masturbation, sex, or love. More on this in a moment.) Learning how to please yourself by yourself increases sexual autonomy and reminds coupled people that their sexuality is theirs and theirs alone; it's not "owned" by a partner. It also helps decrease erotophobia (fear of sex) and increase your overall sexual comfort and self-reliance.

Masturbation can be especially empowering and change making for women. Why? Because their sexuality is often the most shamed and disempowered. Women are often chided for their focus on relationships and for the supposedly more "emotional" way they relate to others. Therapists and doctors disproportionately diagnose them with terms like "codependent" or "love addict" in an effort to discourage them from being hyper-relational. But being hyper-relational is a beautiful thing! We should all be focusing more on our relationships.

Male sexuality, on the other hand, is often publicly perceived as being all about the penis. People forget there are loads of other bodily areas and physical sensations that men can enjoy: nipples, prostates, and butts, to name a few. These are all parts of men's sexual anatomy that, in a lot of heterosexually defined relationships, aren't engaged enough.

LET'S TALK ABOUT PORN

People often ask me whether they're "addicted" to porn simply because they use it to masturbate multiple times per day. The answer is absolutely not! This is standard sex for a lot of people. Sex is a multipurpose tool, and it's absolutely okay to get off as often as you want and to watch porn while doing so.

There's no such thing as porn addiction.

No one has an issue with someone sitting around watching a full day of football or *Real Housewives*, but do the same with masturbation or hooking up and it's seen as an addiction. This is sex phobia (and slut-shaming). It's healthy to spend time focusing on your own pleasure—and not all your time needs to be productive!

Sex is one of the best ways to cope with difficult emotions and stress, and to entertain yourself. If it's healthy to read a book, do yoga, or play basketball with your buddies, it should be the same for sex.

There is no correct number of times to orgasm per day, but the more you do, the stronger your prostate, vaginal muscle tone, and sexual psychology will be. Masturbation plays an important physical function, and it's as valuable for health as lifting weights, getting enough sleep, and proper hydration.

To be sexually healthy, you must first unlearn all that you've been taught in your life about sex, especially the bullshit stigma of masturbation and online porn addiction. The positive benefits of porn use are vast but are often overlooked because so many men have been shamed for their enjoyment of porn and have been led to believe that it is bad for their psychological and physical health, especially their erections. You cannot become *addicted* to porn or masturbation, nor can it cause erectile dysfunction. These myths have been debunked by all the major sexual health and sex therapy organizations.

Masturbation and porn also help save relationships because they give the higher-sex-drive partner another sexual outlet that still honors monogamy. Using porn is not cheating. Porn is actually relationally supportive, as it can help partners with incongruent sex drives or sexual interests find ways to get all their needs met.

Of all the many benefits of masturbation and porn, one of the most powerful is their ability to normalize diverse bodies and sexual interests. But be aware of the types of porn you are watching, and *make sure they lead to higher self-esteem and higher body esteem*. This is part of the concept of surrounding yourself with media that reflects back who and how you want to be. Watch porn that shows diverse bodies, a wide variety of sexual behaviors, and different penis sizes. Body and penis shame exists for many men, and seeing your body type being eroticized is so beneficial for your sexual and psychological health.

CLIENT CASE STUDY

A few years back, a couple came in to see me. "Estella" and "Bill" were very sexually avoidant and had both been raised in a culture that is not very open toward frank expressions of sexuality. For them, sex had always been considered dirty, and they had never experienced sex as a fun, pleasurable outlet. Estella was especially uncomfortable and refused to talk about anything sexual in any capacity, including physical anatomy. She wouldn't use words like *vulva* or *vagina*. She explained that she wanted to get pregnant but felt intense pain any time she and her husband attempted to have sex. Her primary therapeutic goal was to feel less pain solely in order to get pregnant—not because she actually wanted to experience pleasure or have more intimacy with her husband. I told her, "We need to start in a much more elementary way here. Number one: we're going to start by just talking confidently about sex, both at home and in my office, because you can't live authentically or have happy adult relationships if you can't talk about it." Also, if a couple or an individual can't talk about sex, then I don't trust them to talk about other triggering or anxiety-provoking conversations (such as "I don't want to have another child" or "I don't want to move in with your parents"). So if couples can talk about intimate subjects like sexuality and anatomy, I feel confident they can handle other important life topics, too.

Hearing me say words like *vagina* and *vulva* was horrifying for Estella at first. She said she felt like running out of the room. So I didn't immediately tell the couple to go home and watch porn, but they definitely needed some therapeutic sexual intervention. First I told her to head home and look at and touch her own vagina. I know that sounds incredibly basic, like some sort of boring 1972 sex-book crap, but in this case, it was well warranted.

After she mastered these exercises, eventually we got to the point where porn could be integrated into the couple's work. The wife's exposure to confident, healthy sexuality, through specific types of porn I prescribed, helped them develop sexual language as a couple. They could talk about what they were watching: what was arousing and what wasn't. This was a way to pull them together.

Porn is a form of art, and their sharing of it together was like a couple's going to an art show or a movie and discussing what they saw and how it moved them. She was learning how to feel pleasure on her own because you can't do partner's work unless you've learned to handle it yourself first. I also asked them to go to a sex boutique together because for many just the act of walking into a store like that, in front of other people, is a profound experience that represents that sex is okay; we aren't diminished or devalued by prioritizing sex, by being here, by spending our money on sex products. The more she got comfortable with sex, her own body, and their sexuality together as a couple, the more she was able to relax. And once she could truly relax, then penetration was no longer painful—it actually became pleasurable.

For hetero men who may be interested in trying anal penetration (you should!), I recommend trying sex toys on yourself with no shame. A lot of guys don't have confidence asking for anal play from their girlfriends because, again, people make generalizations that if a guy wants something in his butt, he must be gay. Masturbation with vibrators, dildos, and butt plugs is a safe way to explore this sort of play and get comfortable before a partner does it to you with a finger or a strap-on. It's also good for a guy who wants to anally penetrate a girl to first penetrate themselves to help them understand what it feels like, how it should be done, and how slowly they'll need to move (hint: you'll want to move slowly). For men, anal masturbation can be a revolutionary way to learn to engage with their entire body sexually and help them break from the confines of toxic masculinity.

Masturbation also:

- helps sexual assault victims reclaim their power, safety, and pleasure
- offers an avenue for mindful feminist sexuality: a place where women can be sexually assertive and claim their own desires without outside influence
- provides a liberating outlet of self-expression for people who feel sexually repressed or are inexperienced

Therapeutic Uses for Porn

As you've probably noticed by now, I'm a huge advocate for porn. I especially support feminist, queer, body-positive porn that uses all types of faces, body sizes, shapes, and sexualities. Porn, like all forms of art and film, has many different benefits, and how and why we use it determines its value. It bears a stigma from people who are afraid of sex or those who don't appreciate how diverse, broad, and powerful it can be. Plus, plenty of miseducated "experts" have written books warning against the dangers of porn, also creating BS labels like "porn addict" to try to transform simply enjoying erotic movies into some kind of sick disorder. Porn's healing benefits are always omitted from the modern dialogue. But they shouldn't be. Porn helps:

- normalize diverse sex acts
- provide a needed counterbalance to a sex-phobic culture
- determine your authentic sexual interests: it's a safe place to learn and uncover everything that turns you on
- increase esteem for bodies that fall beyond our culture's oppressive beauty standards
- aid couples in finding new ways to be sexual with each other
- provide pleasure and sexual outlets to single people
- provide stress relief
- promote self-soothing
- provide entertainment

Sex Addiction: Is It Real?

For some people, happy, safe, fun sexuality means having a lot of sex with a lot of different people. For others, it means masturbating multiple times a day or watching hours of porn. Yet all these activities can cause someone to be labeled a sex addict. In my world, that's completely wrong. In my world, sex addiction is *absolutely not real.* The entire concept is fraught and questionable at best; it's not an official diagnosis in any way, shape, or form.

In fact, the "sex addict" label didn't come into play until fairly recently and it's far from medically or psychologically legit. The term has been rejected by the *Diagnostic and Statistical Manual of Mental Disorders* (DSM), the American Psychological Association, the American Psychiatric Association, and AASECT (American Association of Sexuality Educators, Counselors, and Therapists). It's only legitimized by those who created a treatment for it and hence make money off of it.

But you'd never know that from mass culture, where the term is thrown around everywhere from doctors' offices to twelve-step programs. "Sex addict" is now a one-size-fits-all label that experts use to shame people who have more sex (or simply different sex) than what's commonly considered "normal." Different is not disordered, remember? If a partner has a higher sex drive than you do, or wants more sex or different types of sex than you feel comfortable with, the solution isn't to just slap them with a "sex addict" label and bail. Having disparate sex drives, kinks, or sexual preferences is often an issue that can be mediated and worked out within a healthy relationship.

Psychological diagnoses aren't unequivocal truths. In fact, they're nothing more than opinions—social constructs that live on a shifting and unsteady continuum. And diagnoses are most oppressive toward sexual minorities—people with creative sex lives and robust sexualities who may not fit the norm. But *tons* of people don't fit into that norm, and lo and behold, not too long ago masturbation, homosexuality, and transgender folks were also shamed and pathologized for their identities. I don't see "sex addiction" as any different, so I don't treat people for it, and I don't support doctors, therapists, or laypeople who use this offensive term or buy into the concept's existence.

There's No Such Thing as "Too Much" Sex

People who like a lot of sex or a lot of porn are also commonly shamed by doctors and therapists for using sex as a tool; for having sex "for the wrong reasons." But who gets to say what a "wrong reason" is? In my professional opinion, sex is a healthy way to engage yourself if you're bored. Sex can help relieve stress. Sex is a healthy coping mechanism. The parts of your brain that are put into play when you're doing yoga or meditation are the same ones that fire when you masturbate.

And there's no reason to deprioritize sex, porn, or masturbation as viable tools to help you feel better when it comes to relieving anxiety, depression, loneliness, and more. If you're told that your only "healthy" or "appropriate" options for relieving stress are going hiking, reading a book, watching a movie, taking a nap, and meditating, but sex and masturbation aren't included on that list, that's sex negativity at work. Why are you allowed to go to the gym to feel good, but not to have sex or touch yourself? Why can you go, without being judged, to a yoga retreat for a weekend to feel emotionally centered and happier within yourself, but not to a sex retreat?

All in all, what's most important when it comes to deepening your own relationship with sexuality is actually *engaging with sexuality*—that is, having sex. So go have sex! Whether that's with yourself, a monogamous partner, or someone new every day of the week is your call. Sure, you'll hit occasional snags and make occasional missteps—the "meh" one-night stands, the broken hearts, the mixed signals. That's part of life. Regardless, your sexual explorations will enrich your life in ways you didn't think possible; you just need to be willing to take the plunge to reap the rewards.

CHAPTER 3 WRAP-UP

MASTURBATION IS HEALTHY, FUN, AND LIFE ENRICHING.

DON'T SLUT-SHAME, JUDGE, OR POLICE OTHER PEOPLE'S SEXUAL ACTIVITY: THAT'S SEX-NEGATIVE.

PORN CAN BE A THERAPEUTIC TOOL.

THERE'S NO SUCH THING AS SEX "FOR THE WRONG REASONS."

SEX ADDICTION DOES NOT EXIST.

GO HAVE SEX!

GOOD SEX IS ETHICAL SEX

Good sex is ethical sex: consensual, compassionate, and honest, without shame or guilt. Whether you're looking for a one-night hookup or the love of your life, it's important to remember that there's a human being on the receiving end of everything you're doing and saying out there—both on the dating apps and between the sheets. No one is just a "trick," a body, or a roll in the hay. They're human beings with hearts, souls, and emotions. All of this needs to stay in the forefront of your mind, no matter what type of sex you're into, or whether you're fucking for intimacy, bonding, procreation, entertainment, comfort, or healing.

Because you're having sex with a person, not an object, it's important to remember that all people have their own issues and preconceptions. Every relationship we enter—every sexual experience, every hookup, every long-term partnership—has the capacity to help us heal *or* to further wound us. Even those seemingly random everyday interactions you have on the sidewalk, at the gas station, or at the coffee shop can accumulate and end up shaping the way you feel about sex and dating. We're relational; even that simple one-minute banter with your local cashier qualifies as a relationship. Our individualistic culture is obsessed with the idea of "everyone for themselves"—but we are *always* embedded in relationships, any time and any place people interact. Ethical dating and sexuality must proceed with a clear awareness of this.

Compassionate Consent: The Core of Good Sex

The foundation for any and every healthy, fun sexual experience is consent. Without it, you simply can't have ethical sex *or* good sex. Without consent, rape culture thrives and sexual abuse continues to flourish. People with minority status have limited power due to outside oppressions (sexism, racism, cissexism, classism, body shame, ableism, etc.). People with privilege often lack a fuller, deeper understanding of consent, because they are more often the ones who cause harm; they haven't been taught to look beyond their bubbles.

Consent is a concept that can and should be instilled early—even in children. Personal boundaries are huge and everyone needs to know how to set these limits. This responsibility falls on parents, but sadly, most of us didn't grow up learning these ideas. Thankfully, as more and more adults are beginning to understand the significance of consent, that's starting to change (albeit slowly). Children should be encouraged to stand up for their own body autonomy (the basic right to control and govern one's body without external influence, pressure, or force).

Sex-positive parenting means helping kids grow up knowing it's okay to touch themselves, explore their bodies, use correct language for their anatomy, and say both yes *and* no when it comes to body boundaries.

Consent and Compassion

Consent sounds simple on the surface—"Did you say yes? Cool, let's have sex"—but it's actually way more complex. Healthy, authentic, ethical sex involves reading someone's body language, not just absorbing their words. If someone said yes to a sex act but doesn't seem to be actively enjoying the act—if they aren't moving, aren't vocalizing, or are expressing displeasure—it's safe to assume they're not into it. Which means you should stop without waiting to be told. Remember, this is a person you're dealing with; it's on you to think about their needs, their pleasure, and how they might feel after the experience.

It's also important to remember that consent can *always* be revoked. It doesn't matter how in love you are; whether you're married, single, with one partner, with four partners, at home in bed, or at an S/M club. There's no commitment on earth that's irrevocable (including marriage). People can change their minds *anytime*, about *anything*—and that can naturally extend to sexual encounters, too. It's perfectly healthy and appropriate to say, "Hey, you know what? Things have changed. I'm no longer interested in this relationship or encounter"—and you can do that in the middle of a sex act. It's your right, and both parties need to honor that: the person saying it and the person hearing it.

Why? Because no one can give blanket consent. No one can say, "Hey, I'm consenting to have sex with you, and that covers anything and everything you might possibly want to do from here on out." Just because someone took off their top doesn't mean they're consenting to take off their pants; just because someone took off their pants doesn't mean they're consenting to penetration. Consent is an ongoing exchange and there are multiple points of verbal or nonverbal acknowledgment that need to occur along the way. Pay attention to the cues someone is giving: both verbal and nonverbal signals of "I want this, this feels good, I'm comfortable, I'm interested."

A healthy, ethical person wants to have sex only with people who are interested in having sex with them. There's the compassion piece again: every time you engage with someone relationally or sexually, in any capacity, even just a brief conversation, you affect them. Every exchange—sexual or otherwise—has the capacity to change a life or influence someone's thinking: to make them feel better and safer in the world in terms of love, sex, dating, and their body or to make them feel worse. I put the responsibility on the reader of this book to care about that.

SEXUAL ASSAULT AND HARASSMENT ARE MEN'S ISSUES

Sexual assault and harassment are most commonly perpetrated by men. For this reason, more men need to commit themselves to caring about the ways in which they participate in rape culture and sexism, not to mention the ways they participate in outright harassment, assault, inappropriate touch, and more. Most important, they have to take accountability. If you feel like you may have hurt someone, admit it. Apologize. Take ownership. Ask what you can do. And most important, educate yourself and commit yourself to never perpetuating or participating in that type of behavior again.

There's No Consent Checklist

I believe in enthusiastic consent, but I also appreciate the nuances of human sexual experiences: no one is holding up a checklist for someone to sign off on every few seconds. So much of sex is non-verbal; again, you need to *look at* the person you're with. Do they look relaxed, comfortable, and engaged? If so, that's a good nonverbal sign that they're enjoying themselves (but again, that doesn't give you the go-ahead to do whatever you want).

After someone gives their consent, it's also helpful to make sure they're fully comfortable and enjoying themselves during a sexual experience by saying things like, "Does that feel good? Do you like it when I touch you here, or kiss you here, or suck you here?" It's healthy sex talk, and a lot of consent-based questions can easily be answered using this type of language. If your partner gives you feedback that nope, they don't enjoy having their left toe sucked, that's good to know, and you can easily stop the action right there.

Conversations about consent might not always feel sexy. But I promise you, having sex in which both parties are 100 percent invested in everything that's happening is 100 times hotter and more fulfilling than the alternative. It's like when people say things such as "Oh, planned sex sounds horrible, it should be spontaneous." Really? That's weird, because you plan exotic beach vacations months in advance, yet those tend to be amazing!

Dear Dr. Chris,

I've gone on a few dates with this girl, and after getting close and spending time together, I don't feel like the chemistry is sufficient for us to keep dating. I've pulled back, started texting her less, and just generally started making myself less available. I'm not doing this to be an asshole; I just don't want to hurt her feelings. I feel bad because she's really cool, but I don't want to wound her, so I'm trying to let her down easy. Should I do something else to let her know I'm not feeling it anymore?

DR. CHRIS: Dating is about spending time together to see if there's chemistry and compatibility. Part of ethical dating is taking responsibility for honestly ending what you start with other people if you learn there is no romantic or sexual chemistry and instead want friendship or no further engagement at all. Slowly spending less time together, making up excuses for not hanging out, texting less, and leaving more time between communications reflect a lack of compassion. Leaving it unclear so your partners have to guess how you feel or what you want is unkind and a sign that you may not be mature enough to date. The kindest thing to do is to give honest and direct communication. Do not use language that may be confusing or allow for hope that you are still interested. This is what will help your partner move on without being angry or resentful.

Informed Consent

Another thing to keep in mind when it comes to ethical sex and dating is the importance of informed consent. People can't properly say yes to something if they don't fully understand what it is they're saying yes to. There has to be clarity up front. Again, I'm not saying you should send a new partner an itemized checklist of all the things you want to do in bed before you meet up; that would be ridiculous, and sex requires some adaptability and flexibility.

Informed consent simply means you're never withholding relevant information from a new partner; if you have an STD, you tell someone up front. If you're in an open or polyamorous relationship, you tell someone up front. If you're only on the market for a one-night stand, you tell someone up front. If someone seems into you, excited about you, and ready to date you or have sex with you, it's your responsibility to do them the courtesy of being truthful about where you're at and what you're looking for. If you're not, there's no informed consent about the relationship parameters, and that's not fair. You can say something like "Hey, just so you know, I know you're down to have sex and that's awesome, but I'm also in an open marriage, so I'm really only available for X, Y, or Z. Is that cool?"

Same goes for dating or simply pursuing someone. If you're interested in someone and you start texting them, it's great if it turns out that they're feeling it, too. Reciprocity is amazing. But if they don't text you back, stop texting you back, or admit they're not ready or interested in dating you, that's your cue to cut and run. Don't pressure them, don't chase them, and for god's sake, don't keep texting them. This is called honoring boundaries. It might feel hard at first—we all want people to like and desire us—but it will get easier the more you do it.

Monogamy Should Not Be Assumed

Monogamy should never be assumed when you've started dating someone. Just because you've started experiencing feelings and fantasies about deleting your dating profiles forever doesn't mean they feel the same or want the same things yet. Don't assume anything until you've heard someone speak the words out loud. The healthiest way to think when you're dating is to assume *the opposite of monogamy* with everyone you meet—assume everyone is dating (and potentially sleeping with) multiple people. If you've met someone you like and you want to be monogamous, talk with them about it and ask if they're on the same page.

ETHICAL TEXTING = HONEST COMMUNICATION

For many, texting is the primary form of building and sustaining relationships these days. But there are plenty of problems involved in it, namely, that so many people use ambiguous language and communication patterns that keep each other confused. When people aren't direct about how they feel and what they want and play games, disappear, or refuse to properly end a budding connection, it leaves daters dealing with pain and disappointment. Oh, and suffice it to say, it's not kind, cool, or ethically sound.

One texting pattern to avoid is *saying just enough to keep the other person around*, when in reality, you're simply not into it. You might be just trying to keep them on ice or to let them down easy. Maybe you're not sure what to say or you're enjoying the attention you've been getting from them. But it's not fair to drag this stuff out when the other person clearly thinks you're into them. Your lack of guts to spell out the truth is cruel and deceptive. Don't make excuses. Don't lie. Don't say, "Oh, I've been really busy this week," when someone asks you why you disappeared for a few days. End things in a compassionate, honest fashion; say, "Sorry I didn't get back to you. I've realized that, as much fun as I've been having with you, we're not really a match." Don't keep them lingering on the line. There's no compassion in that.

The most authentic kind of communication style—the style I'd like everyone reading this book to walk away with the intention of practicing—is to be super-direct and clear. It never leaves the other person guessing; they know whether you're interested or not. And when you're not, you tell them in a kind but honest fashion; you don't drag things out, play games, or beat around the bush.

The absolute worst kind of texting style, when it comes to sex and dating, is the game-playing, manipulative sort practiced by people who just want to have someone around at any cost. They'll lie and mislead you, and they never have the guts to admit when something isn't working out; instead they'll ghost you or feed you a bunch of lies about why they're *totally not ghosting* you (as they're slowly disappearing from your life). Which has happened to me, by the way; I was talking to someone and it was really amazing, deep, and honest—and then all of a sudden they just never responded to me again. An authentic, healthy person would have told me, "It's been really cool getting to know you, but I decided to get serious with someone else," or "I realized the chemistry's no longer there," or whatever. I would have gotten it! But . . . silence. It's the responsibility of the person whose mind has changed to say something about it.

The Ethics of Anonymous Sex

Sure, there's something to be said for sex in which passionate feelings are involved. But anonymous one-night-stand sex can also be one of the most intimate kinds of physical contact you can experience because it's the most honest. It's anonymous, so there are no ties, no baggage, no assumptions, no expectations, no judgments, no social politics. It's literally soul to soul. You don't know who they are. You don't know who their friends are. A one-night stand is exclusively about the pleasure of connection: it's one of the closest, most intimate, most honest types of relationship that someone can have.

So how can you have a safe, healthy, respectful one-time sexual encounter? It goes back to the compassion piece again. A one-night stand is still a person, not just a hookup, a fling, a fuck buddy, or a lay. When we use these terms, we dehumanize people and turn them into objects. Even if they're coming over just to have sex and leave, even if it's in the bathroom of a nightclub, you're still dealing with a person. You still need to be kind. You still need to help your partner feel good—both during the sexual encounter and afterward.

There's no need to exchange pleasantries like names, birthdays, job descriptions, or anything else (unless you really want to); no need to force them into a traditional relationship paradigm. But if you want to text them afterward to let them know you had fun, go for it! And if you see them on the street or out somewhere, smile and be kind; don't ignore them or pretend you don't know who they are. Even just a one-time sexual experience is still an experience; some sort of relationship was formed. And remember that sometimes one-night stands can bleed into long-term friendships, relationships, and more.

So if you do find out something about them that you find valuable or interesting beyond just a sexual connection, ask them about it. Capitalize on it. If they mention hiking and you've always wanted another hiking friend, ask them to go on a hike. There's nothing wrong with a one-night stand turning into a relationship, and you never know what could evolve.

WHAT TO DO WHEN YOU SEE A RECENT HOOKUP

It doesn't have to be weird when you bump into someone you recently hooked up with, but many of us feel awkward when it happens. Still, there's literally no reason that you can't say hi to someone after a session of thumpin' and bumpin'. Yes, even an anonymous one-off is a meeting of humans, and it's not only cool but meaningful and important to honor that you connected with another human being. So let's take a look at compassionate post-hookup etiquette, shall we?

Sex is always a relational and social experience, regardless of whether it's meant as a way to form an ongoing romantic relationship or not. It's not necessarily a commitment to anything more serious, and neither is a friendly hello, but that hello is about being a kind person. My clinical office is full of people wounded by others, and it demonstrates how powerful all human interactions are for each of us.

No one is beyond needing to strive for more kindness, especially in our current political climate.

So what should you do when you see someone you got busy with? Say hi, wave, smile—maybe even acknowledge how you know them ("that was fun!"). It's kind, it's compassionate, and it's proper post-hookup etiquette.

There's no shame in having a sex life, and ignoring people you've been with only perpetuates the idea that sex is shameful, embarrassing, or unrespectable.

App Dating: How to Date without Being a Sexist, Racist, Body-Shaming Jerk

You may have read other books or dating columns that told you to make a list of what you're looking for in a partner before you get out there and start dating. I'm vehemently opposed to this, because our lists of dating and relationship requirements are all written by our ego: the part of us that actually keeps us single, while still saying we want a partnership.

Age appropriateness, height, race, income, weight requirements—all of this is ego, and it's keeping us from love by demanding more, better, newer, nicer. Love does not think in these terms. So toss your list of requirements of what you think you need from a potential love match. Start fresh with each and every swipe. Get rid of your vision-board bullshit and be genuinely open to new people and experiences. We are more than the sum of our parts. You may think you know what you need, but often you don't.

The goal of dating and relationships is to reteach a person about their beauty and worth. You can't date, fuck, or love yourself *or* anyone else if you're harboring sexist, ageist, racist, body-shaming, or fat-phobic baggage. As long as you are promoting a need for a certain age, body type, or race, you are not working on authentic or ethical relationships. You cannot fully love yourself or others if you carry hate toward different types of bodies.

To ethically date, we all need to push ourselves to be not only people who are true to ourselves and what we're looking for, but kind, decent people who don't buy into the larger fanatical culture. Here's how to ethically date online without being a racist, sexist jerk.

DO BE JUDGMENTAL—BUT NOT IN THE USUAL WAYS. You're allowed to make judgments when it comes to who you will and won't date. In fact, we need *more* smart, strong, passionate people out there making judgments on the sex and love front. The twist? I'm not talking about judging people's looks, bodies, outfits, ages, or races (again, all of that is a sign of not having fully accepted yourself, thereby not allowing others to exist as themselves). I'm talking about being confident enough to make bold proclamations about values when it comes to the type of partner and treatment you're looking for. For example, if you want to date someone who has feminist values, don't swipe right on someone who uses the word *ho* in their profile. If you want to be sex-positive, don't refuse to date trans people or get weird when someone tells you they're bi. If you're progressive enough to be reading this book, you need to be progressive enough to put your ethics into action in your love life. Your own integrity and personal value system depend on it.

DON'T BE AGEIST. There's no such thing as age-appropriate (keep it legal, obviously), so next time you're creating an online or app dating profile, try not setting a specific age range. Look for someone who's life-appropriate and value-appropriate: someone who seems to be aligned with who you are, what you're about, and what you're looking for from sex and life. Once you've met in person, you can evaluate whether the sexual chemistry is on point.

DON'T ENGAGE IN SEXUAL RACISM. Everyone has the right to have sex only with people they are attracted to. But to make a list in your dating profile of entire races you aren't attracted to is sexual racism. You are not completely attracted to *everyone* from one race, right? So it's hard to believe that you would not be attracted to *everyone* from another race, too. Leave out the race preferences and don't swipe right on people who include them in their profiles.

DON'T POLICE ANYONE ELSE'S BODY WITH "HEALTHISM." Some profiles will mention wanting someone "fit" or "gym bodied," but what they actually mean is they want to body police you and shame you if you don't look a certain way. Unless you provide lab tests and blood work, no one can tell if you are "healthy" by just looking at you (and please don't assume that simply having abs means you are "fit" or "healthy"). A lot of what we call "healthy eating" and "healthy bodies" are actually disordered eating and conformity. Many of those with standard gym bodies live off energy drinks, genetically modified, hormone-filled meat, and a chemical soup of supplements, so they are not searching for actual health; they are just engaging in fat-shaming and body bigotry. The body is a vehicle, not an achievement.

DON'T ENGAGE IN SEXUAL OR MENTAL HEALTH SHAMING. If someone discloses an STD—or any other kind of health condition—on their profile, don't judge them for it. This goes for mental illness, too. Online profiles are not the place to make others feel bad by promoting your biases or ignorance around sexual health. No sex is safe, and it all comes with risks. Those who knowingly have an STD and are willing to acknowledge it do not deserve your bullshit or shame. Turning down a date with someone who has an STD is misguided and prejudicial.

DON'T SHAME SOMEONE FOR THEIR PAST RELATIONSHIPS. If a match is up-front about being divorced, separated, or having children, don't run and hide—reward them for their honesty! It takes guts to admit to something that others see as "baggage" on dating sites. (Why having exes or kids is considered baggage is beyond me.) Having a past doesn't reveal anything about someone's future. And being divorced is the same thing as being single: both mean the person has had past relationships (it's just that for the divorced person, the relationship became a marriage). And no matter what kind of relationship you find yourself in thanks to your adventures in online dating—monogamous, open, poly, "fuck buddy," the possibilities are endless—the fundamentals of health are the same.

ONLINE DATING BURNOUT IS REAL

Online dating increases your exposure to a multitude of potential partners; it's cool that way. But it can be both liberating and complicated when it comes to ramifications for your mental health and happiness. One of the biggest dangers of avid Internet dating is burnout: trying to gain traction with each new person can feel harder and more disappointing each time it doesn't click. If you notice yourself getting frustrated, angry, or depressed, take a break. Online/app dating will always be there, and it's meant to enhance your life, not detract from it.

CLIENT CASE STUDY

"John" came into therapy to work with me on his chronic relational problems. He had never had what he would call a "real" relationship, only casual dating and hookups. John said he wanted to explore why he never "gets the guy" like many of his other friends do. One initial red flag I noticed immediately was John's belief that only committed or monogamous relationships are "real"—I told him this was part of what was keeping him single despite his desire for partnership. I explained to him that flings, one-time bangs, and random dates are their own forms of "real" relationships, too, and that these forms of intimacy can and do lead to *more intimacy* and increased levels of commitment.

We worked on exploring how less physical forms of intimacy building, like conversation over coffee or dinner, and more physical kinds, like a hookup, are different, while acknowledging that they both have legitimate value and can lead to something deeper. John had to unlearn what he had been taught, as well as stop dismissing people who lead with sex as being not "husband material" (that is, not open to serious relationships). That not only kept him single and out of relationships but also prevented him from making some amazing new friends.

The next step in our therapy was to examine the specific ways he shut out meeting someone compatible for him. I had John take out his phone and we carefully looked through his online dating profiles and how he marketed himself. We evaluated the messages his posted pictures communicated, and also what he listed as wanting in a partner, where these desired qualities in a partner came from, if they were authentic, and how they would work for and against him. We removed specifics that kept him from staying open enough to match with someone and explore true chemistry.

Age, career, height, weight: all promise nothing about actual compatibility or chemistry. I worked with John on truly aligning his behavior with his goal of partnership. Both ignoring people who didn't meet his arbitrary qualifications and claiming one fixed, inflexible sexuality (John came in saying he would partner only with a "top") kept him perpetually single and looking. Unpacking his rigidity about relationships and loosening his grip on what he deemed "respectable" enough to pursue allowed John to have more fun, make new friends if the romantic chemistry was lacking, and see more possibilities for love in his future. This all obviously led to more happiness and higher quality of life.

Breakups Suck—and They're Unavoidable

Many relationships don't last a lifetime, and the idea that it might last forever should never be the standard assumption when entering one. Breakups can be painful, but they're an unavoidable part of dating and being vulnerable, regardless of whether you've been out with someone three times or three hundred.

I don't like using the word *breakup*, though we'll use it in this book for clarity's sake. A healthy relationship isn't determined by the length of time it spans, and realizing a relationship has run its course doesn't have to be a miserable or tragic thing. It's about redefining a commitment, shifting boundaries, and developing new, different identities than the one you shared as a couple.

If you need to end a relationship, here are some guiding principles to remember:

SHOW COMPASSION. Again, remember that you're ending a relationship with a *person*. No matter how ugly things got or how disappointed you may feel, maintain your high ground and treat the other person with respect, dignity, and humanity. Exit with integrity!

DON'T BURN IT ALL DOWN. Staying friends with your exes is a healthy sign, but that doesn't mean it's always possible. I've had messy breakups in which it wasn't all sunshine and rainbows, and I didn't feel comfortable high-fiving my ex if I saw them at the gym or whatever. That's fine, but try to maintain some level of respect, kindness, and warmth between you, for both of your sakes.

DON'T TALK SHIT. Publicly talking ill of an ex says more about you than them. When you bash your ex, you're telling everyone you see that you're unsafe to date. In effect, you're saying, "If you disappoint me or let me down, I'll do this to you as well." Don't be that person because you're just red-flagging yourself for the world.

UNFOLLOW YOUR EX. Unfollow your ex on social media. Otherwise you won't get over them. Seeing their posts on Instagram and Twitter every day keeps them at the forefront of your mind emotionally and psychologically, which does not help you move on. You can always go back and add them later if you get to a point where that's comfortable.

EXPECT SOME IDENTITY DISRUPTION. Expect to feel some initial confusion, sadness, and alienation after parting ways with a partner. You'll have to reform your identity as a single person and ask yourself, "Who am I when I'm single?" This is a normal and natural part of the process. Let yourself find both old and new hobbies, friends, activities, and interests.

STAY OPEN TO THE HURT. You are wounded. We don't treat emotional wounds with the same respect we give physical wounds (for instance, your boss will better understand the special needs of a broken leg than those of a broken heart), but *you* have to. Ask for what you need and honor that you do have an injury.

LEARN FROM IT. Prior relationships can reveal patterns and relational issues we might have. Looking back at our relationship flaws can help us learn to do things differently next time.

DON'T AVOID YOUR FEELINGS. Self-care is hugely important immediately after a relationship ends. Eat well, sleep well, exercise to help with stress, and socialize with friends to help preserve your peace of mind and find your emotional footing again.

GET BACK OUT THERE. Start dating as soon as possible. The length of time you wait between relationships does not say anything about the success or health of the next relationship. As I discussed earlier, a rebound is not a real thing, so I recommend clients get back to dating fairly quickly if a relationship is what they really want. Just be careful about not projecting old issues onto new partners. Remember, this is a whole new person; don't see them as your ex or hold them accountable for stuff your ex did.

HOW DO YOU KNOW WHEN YOU'RE READY TO DATE AGAIN?

It's easy: you'll feel ready to date again! Ideally you'll also feel a shift in the way you view the relationship you left. You'll have:

- forgiven your ex for whatever transgressions or hurts took place
- found a sense of gratitude and acknowledged that the partnership helped you grow
- found some personal happiness and built a life you like

Don't look to a relationship to make you happy. Get happy first!

There are no ways to accelerate or rush through these steps, by the way. They happen at a different pace for everyone. But I don't suggest waiting too long to get back out there and date again. Sometimes healing happens with the help of a new partner.

Taking more or less time between relationships does not predict how long the next relationship will last—and getting involved sooner rather than later can help you feel happier and more confident in your desirability. It could also help you get over any residual feelings for your ex. Remember, there's no such thing as a rebound relationship; all relationships are just . . . relationships, standing individually, on their own merits.

Sexting Etiquette and Revenge Porn

It saddens me that we still have a culture of shame around naked bodies and healthy adults sexting each other, but we do. I'll discuss more specifics on how to be a good sexter elsewhere in this book. For this chapter's purposes, I want to discuss the ethics of sending and receiving naked photos with people you're dating or talking to. You need to be careful and compassionate when dealing with these kinds of pictures.

Most states now have revenge porn laws, which means two very important things: (1) it is illegal to post naked pics that are not of you and that you do not own; (2) just because someone sent you naked pics of themselves does not mean you now own those pics. Sending you pics is not transferring ownership to you. If someone posts or shares pics of you without your consent, ask for their removal and contact the police.

The ethical thing to do is to not post, share, or resend anyone else's photos. I also recommend deleting the pics after a certain length of time. Honor the reason they were sent to you: for sexual reasons in one specific moment—to build intimacy, to arouse, or to feel closer. Then delete them after you've looked at them. The blame for anything else occurring with those pics falls on the receiver, not the sender (though of course people tend to slut-shame the sender).

If you feel nervous but you still want to sext, then crop out your face in your pics and vids, as well as any other distinguishing features.

Compassion is the key to a healthy, happy sex and dating life. If you're a kind, decent person in every other area of life but you consistently push people beyond their sexual limits, play texting games, or ghost people, you need to take some time to reflect and work on yourself. Remember, our sex lives reflect the health of our entire lives. How we treat people really matters. So be better and care more! The rest of your life will improve for it.

CHAPTER 4 WRAP-UP

CONSENT IS THE CRUX OF GOOD SEX.

DON'T ASSUME EVERYONE IS—OR WANTS TO BE—MONOGAMOUS.

ETHICAL TEXTING IS ABOUT CLEAR AND HONEST COMMUNICATION.

BE COMPASSIONATE DURING BREAKUPS; DON'T BURN IT ALL DOWN!

IF YOU'RE SEXTING AND SENDING OR RECEIVING NAKED PHOTOS, BE CAREFUL— REVENGE PORN LAWS MAY COME INTO PLAY.

GHOSTING SOMEONE IS NEVER OKAY.

ANONYMOUS SEX CAN BE FUN AND POWERFUL, BUT DON'T IGNORE A ONE- NIGHT-STAND PARTNER IF YOU SEE THEM AFTERWARD.

ALL BODIES ARE BEACH BODIES

Being a human in this day and age is tough. If you're anything like my clients and me, you've probably spent a fair share of your time on this planet muddling through toxic ideas about how your body should look, feel, and behave. Why? Because mainstream culture is beholden to industries that profit from keeping us on a perpetual quest for insecurity-driven self-improvement. Think about all the industries that would shut down if we all actually loved—or at least *accepted*—our bodies the way they are now instead of how they could conceivably be a few years (or a few pounds) down the road.

Instead of being shamed for not being perfect, you'd be told "wear what you want," "all bodies are beach bodies," "health at every size," and "fat is hot." But in our current culture, the simple act of liking your own body—or at least not actively striving to change it—is a powerful form of resistance. We've been taught to be oppositional with our bodies. We haven't been shown how to love them and be truly *in* them. "Looking good" isn't taking care of or loving your body; it's ego and conformity. True body love is internal, not external—and *your* body—is for *your* pleasure. Its goal is not to look good for others. The work is to go inward and focus less on the outside. Think about how you feel, not how you look.

In the eyes of the diet industry, there's no such thing as too thin. In the eyes of the fitness industry, fat is always bad, lack of muscle is gross, and your worth is dependent on meeting a body standard you never signed up for in the first place. In the eyes of the beauty industry, you're past your prime on your thirtieth birthday, after which you're shamed and blamed for succumbing to the healthy aging process.

Are You Hot Enough to Have Sex?

That's the sinister question lurking behind so much of the media we consume. Entire industries are built on the idea that we need to somehow prepare ourselves for sex—get our bodies fit at the gym, the salon, the waxer, whatever. We keep getting told that looking good and feeling good is the path to being desirable and getting action. But this couldn't be further from the truth! In fact, it's the opposite: sex is actually your path toward self-love and greater body esteem, especially for people with nonnormative bodies (that is, the ones that fitness calls unhealthy, fashion calls fat, beauty calls old, and media calls ugly).

Our brains are social organs. Each interaction with another person shifts our self-esteem either closer to feeling more desirable and confident or away from a sense of worth and value. So every time you have sex, your brain is neurologically reorganized. This is why having sex is never *just* sex.

Body shame is what holds many of us back, and it is an especially powerful deterrent to sex for those who don't fit into the young, white, thin, able-bodied, hung categories. But the idea that this is what is *naturally* desirable over anything else is, well, bullshit.

For years we've been peddled a cookie-cutter mold for what the general population considers to be of a high sexual value. But there are many spaces where culturally nonnormative bodies are actually eroticized and prioritized.

So go where your desirability is highest, and socialize with people who value your body type, too. Having your fuckability reflected back to you heals you and boosts your sense of worth. Don't exclusively hang out at bars or other social events where you are marginalized erotically.

But, more powerfully, seek out sex! Sexual arousal lessens inhibitions, so getting turned on from sex can actually reduce the anxiety of being naked with someone else, while simultaneously reinforcing that you're wanted, hot, and desirable on your own.

And doing it over and over will reduce the anxiety accompanying new behaviors and partners. Our arousal is malleable—we have some control over what we find arousing based on what we pair with our orgasms. Remember, porn has a huge impact on what we view as arousing, including our own bodies. So what you choose to watch in your solo sex life matters, too. Seek out porn that shows your body type so you can see it eroticized—both giving and getting pleasure.

Until there is a cultural shift on what we reinforce as attractive and hot and we begin to consider all bodies erotic, the work falls on each of us to use sexuality as part of our healing, and not against ourselves.

Though it's hard to quiet this external media assault, no one is *forcing* us to buy into these ideals. It's on us to challenge ourselves when it comes to our self-image. And having counseled thousands of individuals through a boundless variety of relationship and personal predicaments, I can tell you for a fact: the most revolutionary thing you can do—for yourself, for your sex life, and as an example for the rest of the world—is to learn to celebrate your own body exactly as it is now. Here are a few ways you can start doing that.

Reject Diet and Exercise

If you're going to work out, it shouldn't be to lose weight. It shouldn't be to look "hot," get abs, or start resembling a supermodel. If working out causes your body to release endorphins and gives you a healthier frame of mind, if it's something you enjoy simply for its own sake, then great! Lots of people feel that way, but many of them don't. Your most critical mission when it comes to your physical being is *body acceptance*, no matter what size you are now.

Body acceptance—as well as its sister issue, fat acceptance—isn't some niche feminist catchphrase. It affects everyone, because all systems of oppression feed into each other. Sexism, racism, fat phobia: they're all connected. And every time you criticize a body—including your own!—you're telling people they don't have a right to exist, that their bodies are wrong, that they don't deserve the happiness, love, and sexual satisfaction we all strive for. You're reinforcing the idea that there's one right way to look and be.

As a human in this culture, none of us can escape some degree of dysmorphia; we all live in a gross self-improvement culture. But here's a new mantra I want you to start practicing: *My body is not an achievement.* Because it's true. Your worth is not tied to what you ate for dinner last night. You weren't "good" if you had salad and "bad" if you had an ice cream sundae. There's no glory in losing weight or working out a lot. You should be exercising for vascular health, stress relief, and pleasure.

Stop Talking about Your Body

If you want a healthier relationship with your body, stop talking about your body. I know that sounds strange, but hear me out. To stop the obsession with looking a certain way, make a personal commitment to stop discussing your juice fast, or how much pizza you ate yesterday, or how you'd feel "cuter" if you were fitter, thinner, or more toned. Stop talking about your gym routine, your plans for your next marathon, and your weight goals. Stop making your body a topic of discussion!

All these subjects are destructive. They keep you focused on the external, on the idea that your contentment and worth are inseparable from your body shape. You are more than your body! You can't have a healthy body image *or* a healthy mind if you're monitoring every calorie that goes in and out. Act as if talking about food, weight, and body stuff is 100 percent off-limits. It will help you and everyone around you, too.

Stop Telling People What to Wear

Stop telling people what's "flattering" on them. Every time someone says "dress for your size," it's a small act of cruelty, implying that someone is "less than" for not fitting the common physical ideal. Those small cruelties compound and can eventually work to crush someone's self-image.

For example, one of my clients, a young woman, came in to see me complaining that she didn't know what was wrong, exactly, but that *something* was. She said she felt fat, ugly, and unworthy. For her whole life, her mother and other relatives had been encouraging her to stick to oppressive rules about what she "could" and "couldn't" wear as a bigger girl: no horizontal stripes, no above-the-knee skirts, no knee-high boots because they'd make her calves look "thick." She was in her twenties by the time she visited my office, and as an adult she'd swapped her family's oppressive influence for that of social media and fashion magazines.

She was perpetually single because going on dates made her so nervous; she hated displaying her photos on dating apps. Most therapists would've told her, "Let's look at your childhood for answers about why you never felt good about yourself." And while her family input certainly played a part in shaping her views about her body, I believe the general culture played a bigger part. I told her to stop questioning and start dating—*now*. I told her to wear whatever made her comfortable on those dates. She had to practice acting like she was worthy until eventually she began believing it. She didn't need to change anything except the way she was talking to and about herself. When she stopped waiting for some future "real life" to begin, when she decided she was good enough as she was *right that moment* and began putting herself out there, she grew more and more comfortable with who she was and what she deserved. And yes, eventually she met a great partner.

CLIENT CASE STUDY

I work with a variety of clients who are fat-identified. One of these clients—I'll call her "Kelly"—was struggling with her levels of sexual confidence. She felt "meh" in the everyday world and her lack of body confidence was hindering her love and sex life. As we began exploring those issues in depth, I asked her to watch porn involving fat bodies, to unfollow any social media accounts that made her feel bad about herself (fitness and thinspiration accounts were nixed), and to try using online dating photos that *celebrated* her body size and shape instead of hiding it.

After a couple of months, things began to quietly shift for Kelly, and she started attracting a handful of new dates and partners. This boosted her confidence, emboldening her to make healthier choices in other areas of her life, too. She went back to school for an advanced degree, and is currently in a beautiful, healthy, long-term relationship with someone great. The effects of working on her sexual confidence and body image fanned out into every aspect of her life, but what I asked her to do was, in some ways, the antithesis of what most self-help books would suggest. I didn't tell her to post only the "most flattering" photos on her Bumble profile. I didn't tell her to lose weight, or wear different clothes, or be less demanding, or stop wanting what she wanted. In fact, she didn't change anything about herself; she simply shifted her focus to authenticity and self-acceptance, and she eventually attracted someone healthy who accepted her for who she was.

Take a Class, Masturbate, Read a Book

So many of us devote so much time to reforming our bodies: food, gym, antiaging potions, new clothes. But we devote far less effort to reforming our minds and our sexualities: reading, philosophizing, learning, growing. Instead of sitting around on social media tracking other people's #FitnessGoals, do something to help yourself grow internally. Do something you've never done before. You'll feel healthier and happier when you shift your focus from what you're eating and how your body looks to what you do and how you think.

The soul and mind are our most underdeveloped body parts, especially today. Back in the nineteenth century, singles were more focused on personality and character. A higher priority was placed on being decent—building families, working in the community, and forming partnerships. There were a lot of unhealthy rules and restrictions, too, of course. But it's such a shame that, over the years, most people's focus has shifted from character development to superficial bullshit. Nowadays people are trained to focus on being thin and attractive, as well as coupling up and making money. But attractiveness is fickle, and trends change from year to year and culture to culture. Your body does not represent who you are—your character does.

Normal Is Not the Goal

The power of "the average" is great. You are told not to be low energy (depressed) or high energy (ADHD, manic) but to be in the middle: the norm. You are also told not to be too relational (codependent or love addict), too single (avoidant), or too sexually driven and sexually confident (sex addict). Don't be too old (antiaging, always!) or too young (immature), or too fat or too skinny. We don't allow anyone to just be okay as they are. All this behavior involves seeking approval, because our culture demands it. Instead, go the opposite route! Choose the radical act of liking yourself as you are, and don't trade authenticity for approval.

Don't Date Body-Shamers—or Even Body Obsessives

Don't indulge people who are body-shamers or even people who are hyper-body-conscious, because this only presents more challenges when it comes to accepting *your own* body. People who talk a lot about fitness and food will only project their own body policing onto you, keeping you hostage in the "body as achievement" mentality. For example, I don't let people around me discuss their bodies—*or* my body. If they do, I say something like "I'm getting uncomfortable with the way you're talking here," just like I would if someone was having a racist or sexist conversation. Sorry, but I don't want to hear about your ab routine!

I'll also test new people I'm dating by saying things like "I'm taking a break from the gym for a few months because I want to put my energy into something else." If they start to panic—"Skip the gym? For months at a time?"—I know this won't be a healthy relationship for me. I don't want someone's interest in me to be locked into my current body shape or size, because that's inevitably going to shift. We're all going to age and our looks will change.

I'd also tell people to have more sex. Body shame is maintained when you hide—from being sexual, from dating, and from putting your body out there. Having your desirability reflected back to you from a sex partner heals and increases your sense of worth. Sexual arousal is disinhibiting, so the arousal from sex can reduce the anxiety of being naked with another person. Date at the weight you're currently at—and find the people who are attracted to your body as it is right now.

Challenge Your Sexual "Ideal"

Body-shaming is everywhere, not just in media or medicine. I see it in dating, too. People have such rigid expectations and self-defined requirements when it comes to what they find arousing. The thing is, what turns us on isn't as individual as we'd like to think it is. A lot of it is simply internalization of cultural norms. Sizism is one of the last socially acceptable forms of oppression, and I see handfuls of clients who struggle with it every day.

What we find attractive is culturally driven. Instead of being supported in an ongoing journey of erotic exploration, we are shamed and limited at every stage of our lives. Fear of being called a sex addict, a made-up term that shames hypersexuality, suppresses our desire. Sexual orientation labels box us in and prevent us from exploring a wider spectrum of sexual experience. Some parts of the gay community fail to allow the eroticization of the female body, instead engaging in negative, even misogynist talk ("Ew! Vaginas are icky!"). Biphobia dismisses bi men as living in the closet. Slut-shaming leaves people who enjoy sex feeling bad about being a "ho" or not being "boyfriend material."

Add to that how being small and thin is the feminine "ideal" while being big and buff is held up as a standard for men; that's the nonsense the media and fashion/beauty/fitness industries have been shoving down our throats for the past fifty years. These industries are getting rich off marketing those images, and it's on us to challenge our own perceptions of "hot." We should all be pushing ourselves beyond our comfort zones when it comes to dating and sex, and that includes dating people with different bodies than we've typically gone for.

I don't expect everyone to have a dramatic personal shift, and I would never tell someone to have sex with or date someone they weren't attracted to. But we need to hold each other responsible for what we support and reinforce culturally, and that applies to whom we date. If you only date skinny nineteen-year-olds, you're making a statement about desirability and who is worth wanting. That influence will trickle down. Your sister or cousin or friends' kids will see it. You're reinforcing an old and destructive status quo.

HOW TO EMBRACE YOUR BODY

- **UNFOLLOW MEDIA THAT MAKES YOU FEEL BAD ABOUT YOURSELF IN ANY WAY.** That means Instagram, magazines, websites, models, Facebook, Twitter, all the media. Recently at Amber Rose's Slut Walk, three different girls came up to tell me that they'd listened to the podcast and that they'd taken my advice and unfollowed body-negative inspiration and fitness accounts. All three said it had a dramatic effect on how they saw themselves, that their sense of self was no longer so intimately tied to how they looked. For some, body positivity means posting selfies and body or outfit pics; for others, it will mean unfollowing these people.

- **CHALLENGE YOUR LIMIT WHEN IT COMES TO THE CONVERSATIONS YOU'LL ALLOW PEOPLE TO HAVE AROUND YOU.** Don't let people pull you out of wherever you were in your head, in your mood, or in your day and force you to examine your body just because they're dissecting theirs. Walk away.

- **DON'T ALLOW PEOPLE TO COMMENT ON YOUR BODY.** Recently I was on set for a TV show, and the producer kept talking about how "fit" I was. I knew he meant it as a compliment, but it didn't feel that way. Saying those kinds of things is actually cruel in its own way, because it's trapping you and holding you hostage in the way you look right now. Essentially it means you need to stay exactly the way you are right now if you want to keep being valued and loved.

- **WEAR THINGS THAT ACCENTUATE YOUR ENTIRE BODY.** Don't hide your "problem parts." There's no such thing as a problem part! Shame is maintained by hiding. The small act of wearing a crop top can serve as a major path toward sexual expression and liberation for a fat person who's always been told to hide their stomach. It's a fucking stomach! Hiding your body only serves to support the idea that certain body shapes should be allowed to exist.

- **HAVE MORE SEX.** Build more sexuality time into your daily life. Masturbate. Make yourself comfortable being seen naked and observing someone become aroused by how you look. Watch porn that stars similarly sized actors with bodies that are utterly desired and admired by their costars.

- **DON'T READ TRADITIONAL SELF-HELP.** These books actually try to make you feel more broken, more "unacceptable." Their sole aim is selling you products and dishing out tired rules instead of encouraging you to be yourself, the way you are right now. (Also, ironically, these books wouldn't sell at all if you felt okay with yourself.)

Don't Knock It Until You've Tried It

When it comes to dating, practice holding your own physical preferences a little looser. You can't rule out an entire segment of society and say, "I'd never date someone without a six-pack," or "I'd never date someone who wasn't white." That's not realistic, because I know you wouldn't date every single fit white person who stumbled across your path, either. Hold space for surprising yourself with what you find attractive. Follow my rule: when you're doing—or dating—something new, try it at least three times before you write it off.

And when you're talking about people you're dating, never label someone undesirable, unattractive, or "ugly." Just because you're not into them doesn't mean they're unfuckable. Don't reinforce the idea that there are certain people, or certain "types," who aren't worthy of romantic or sexual attention.

What you see as your innate sexual orientation is most likely a watered-down version of your authentic sexuality. In a sexually and socially healthy culture, sexuality would exist in a more open and expansive way, with fewer labels. As we've discussed elsewhere, labels lead to rules and expectations, as well as outright discrimination. Healthy sex is fluid and it allows for a multitude of experiences, ones that may push you outside the boundaries of who you thought you were. Our sex lives are often based on comfort and consistency; we engage in sex that is familiar to us, not what is most arousing. Our arousal systems also change over time.

Be open to trying new things, and more important, to trying them more than once! If we remain open to newness, our sexualities will expand and incorporate a wealth of new pleasure triggers. This is how sex can be kept fun and novel. New partners who love and appreciate your body exactly as it is now—or new experiences with current partners—are prime opportunities to expand your sexuality and enhance how you feel about your body.

Use Social Media Wisely

Mental health isn't just about your thinking; it's also heavily influenced by what you feed your brain *and* your psyche. This includes books, movies, TV shows, and social media; they all play a part in how we feel about our bodies and our lives. The good news is that we have a choice: we *choose* the TV we watch, the music we listen to, the books we read, the social media we follow, and the friends we let into our lives.

The problem is that most media and social media actively work to kill authenticity by sending us messages that we aren't enough as we are—that we need to buy more, eat less, exercise more, and invest in beauty and fashion shit we don't need in order to be lovable and happy. All this negative messaging eventually leads to brainwashed "adults" who are unable to think for themselves; instead of forging their own paths and questioning what they've been told, most people buy into regurgitated norms and values that hold all of us hostage, even if we manage to look or act the "right" way. Our bodies are not public property for commentary and fixing.

There was a time when family, school, and peers were our biggest socializers, though television has always had a huge impact, too, because of its intrinsic tie with marketing and advertising. The entire goal of advertising is, again, to make you feel like you need something outside yourself: that you're not enough as you are, and you need to shell out money on objects or experiences to make your life better.

Social media like Twitter, Instagram, and Facebook showed up much later, of course, and in some ways these forums are way more powerful than the old guard of advertising, television, and printed media. Why? Because social media is *always with you*, unlike TV, magazines, and films. Your cell phone has made the siren call of social media available to you all hours of the day and night, whether you're just waiting in line at a café, sitting bored in class, or trying to fall asleep at home. Even when you're immersed in conversation, a movie, or a book, the lure of the phone is there, and it can be very difficult to ignore.

For this reason, we need to watch ourselves when it comes to the social media we choose to ingest—we're ingesting it for hours a day, and so much of social media reflects the problematic values of our culture. Celebrities have great power through social media, and they often reinforce toxic values on bodies, sex, and dating. Many of today's biggest stars aren't stars because they've contributed anything of artistic value—they're just Instagram stars, YouTube stars, or whatever, making lots of money in sponsorship deals to look and dress a certain way.

Diverse people with nonnormative identities, sexualities, and bodies are all over social media, but they aren't heralded the way so many others are (all those fitspiration accounts? ugh). I've told my clients, "If you hand me your phone right now, I can tell you what's in your psyche just by sifting through your social media accounts. I can tell you how healthy you are. I can assess your level of anxiety and depression based on what you're following and how much you align or don't align with it." If you're following people and accounts that don't reflect back who you are or who you want to be, you're not going to feel acceptable in the world.

My rule: unfollow anything that makes you feel shitty about yourself. Social media should be a source of happiness—not jealousy, shame, guilt, comparison, or pain. Your social accounts should make you smile. This means, for many of us, not following fitspo/thinspo accounts or beauty/fashion accounts that only show off one type of person, skin color, body type, or look. These are not inspiration—they're desperation! Personally, I unfollow everything that doesn't reflect back how I want to think about bodies, culture, or sex; now I exclusively follow folks who reflect healthy norms and the kind of lifestyle I believe in and want to perpetuate: radical self-acceptance, sex positivity, feminism, racial diversity, and gender fluidity.

Oh, and those ads that occasionally pop up in your feed? Fuck them. Even if you don't follow destructive fitspo-type accounts, you still might occasionally get an ad for something horrible—I recently saw the hideous tagline "no pecs, no sex." When you see ads, memes, or slogans like this, challenge them! Your healing relies on it. You need to push yourself to push back against these toxic norms. So if you see an ad or notice a link to a toxic article floating around your FB feed, don't click on it. Unfollow the company, then e-mail them and tell them why you're unfollowing them.

You can also publicly shame them by calling them out on their page or leaving a comment on their post. Tell them you don't support ageism, racism, body-shaming, or antifeminist rhetoric, whatever the offensive case may be (something like "This is really oppressive to me because I struggle with body image issues; you're telling me that my body's unacceptable and that I have to wear or do X, Y, or Z to be okay." Spread the word to your friends to stop supporting those companies and sites, too. In this day and age, we should *all* be activists, even if it's the kind of activism you can do from your couch.

Social Media Isn't All Bad, Though

Social media can also be used for good, of course. There are people (like, um, me) using their pages to promote self-love, authenticity, legit self-care, and the normalization of diversity. It's also important to remember that doing this work isn't just about *accepting* diversity: it's also about actively celebrating and promoting other bodies, looks, ages, races, and sexualities. I don't just accept or tolerate different bodies and sexualities—I celebrate them. And you should, too. Find the people who are putting positive images and words into the world and help spread their message. Make your own platform a haven for body positivity and healthy values, too; create the kind of page you'd be excited to stumble upon.

GENITAL PRIDE

Just as we inhabit a culture that shames people for being too fat, too thin, too short, too tall, too *whatever*, we live in a culture that shames people for having the "wrong" kind of genitals. Men and women both deal with this—way too many people are walking around wondering whether they're "normal" down below. So many of us have no exposure to the true diversity of genitals out there. Other than with a partner, we only see other penises, vaginas, and vulvas in porn.

But heads up: even though mass culture, sex apps, and porn might make you think otherwise, there are no "bad" or "ugly" genitals out there. Porn has tons of benefits, but it's majorly flawed in its lack of diverse penis and vulva representations. To change this, seek out and support body-positive porn— porn that won't harm your genital confidence.

One of the top therapeutic uses for porn is to help you find new ways to be sexual and to boost your arousal levels. Just don't let porn work against you!

The benefits only really kick in if you surround yourself with media that reflects back who you want to be. Watch porn that shows diverse bodies, a wide variety of sexual behaviors, and different-sized penises. Penis shame exists for many men, and seeing smaller penises causing arousal and being eroticized is amazing for your sexual and psychological health.

Your ideas about how things should be, such as the functioning of your penis, are not determined or controlled by you. You have internalized a vision that you are held hostage by. There is an idea that if a penis is not big, erect on demand, or hard for as long as you want, it is a disordered penis needing a cure, help, or fixing. This is toxic masculinity, because a man's worth isn't his genitals. Not all men have a penis, and this also stigmatizes the bodies of those who are intersex. But more important, don't reduce a person to their body. My advice to those who complain that their partner's penis is "too small" or doesn't "stay hard" is to go buy a dildo.

Sometimes dicks that are bigger can feel better (fill and stretch us), but there are things a smaller penis can do better (it nails the prostate and the G-spot far better than a larger cock). Being good in bed means being creative, and when an erection isn't available or a penis isn't your desired size, then sex should become about tongues, fingers, and toys—the hot sex trifecta. Because, FYI to the younger guys, erectile issues are to be expected as you age.

Dear Dr. Chris,

I'm an eighteen-year-old fat girl with anxiety and mild depression. I really want a girlfriend, but I haven't had much luck meeting women in my town; growing up I was always ostracized because of my weight. Social media only seems to make things harder—whenever I check Instagram or Twitter, I start drowning in comparison and insecurity about what everyone else is doing and how happy they appear in their relationships. I know a lot of this is probably not true; it might just be the happy face they're choosing to present to the world, but I end up taking it personally and it makes me feel unloved and alone. Should I turn my phone off? Delete my social apps? What can I do to work on these feelings and find someone to love me as I am?

DR. CHRIS: I generally don't tell anyone to turn off their phones or delete their social media accounts, because that's just not realistic. Everyone should absolutely trash their fashion magazines, though! But instead of limiting your cell phone exposure, just go ahead and unfollow everything and everyone who make you feel bad. Your phone can become a source of happiness if you follow accounts and people who make you feel good by promoting various body shapes, sizes, and sexual identities. A good place to start is fourth-wave feminist accounts; fourth-wave feminism is so important because it's pro-porn, it's pro–body positivity, it's technologically driven, it's art driven, it's political, and it's not gendered.

As far as the insecurity piece goes, I get it; we all go through it in various ways. But remember, this culture—especially certain industries, like diet, fashion, and beauty—*wants* you to feel like shit about yourself. It makes money off your self-hatred. Also, your belief that you're somehow "unacceptable" or unlovable as you are helps keep you quiet, subservient, and unaware of your own power. Believing you're unacceptable is a form of submission and obedience to a handful of oppressive industries that have no respect or investment in your true happiness or health. Liking yourself as you are, whether that's fat, sex obsessed, crazy, loud, fast, anxious, or low energy, is a true form of social resistance. It's actually a radical move to like yourself (and be sexual) just as you are, in any way that turns you on. Try downloading some dating apps and putting yourself out there a little more if you actively want to meet more women. Just don't hold back about the truth of who you are—physically, mentally, and emotionally. There are people out there who will love you for it.

IF SOCIAL MEDIA CAUSED DISORDERS, SOME OF THEM WOULD BE . . .

- **MIPD (MEDIA-INSPIRED PERSONALITY DISORDER):** Those who suffer from this condition follow and obsess about celebrities and "personalities" who promote classism, body shame, and poor mental health behavior. They believe that these celebrities' actions are things to be emulated, that one must follow suit and adopt some of their behaviors in order to be "fabulous" and lovable. We are better served by promoting values attached to accomplishments, character, and relational ability. Many celebs lead the cultural obsession with body policing. Lots of celebs seem to sustain or at least reflect the worst value system: that you are not enough and that you need to wear certain fashions and have a certain body type to be sexy.

- **CTPD (CULTURALLY TRANSMITTED PERSONALITY DIS-ORDER):** This one goes beyond mere famous folks or Insta celebrities; this one seeps in to all of us, all the time, from the world around us. We have to resist and fight back against the social messaging from advertising, magazines, our peers, doctors, and more that tell us our bodies aren't perfect as we are. Gym culture, fitness culture, antiaging culture, makeup, fashion, and so on: I'm looking at you! Personal esteem is based upon way more than how one looks; it's about connection and generosity.

- **AAD (AUTHENTICITY AVOIDANCE DISORDER):** This consists of the belief that you are not perfect as you already are—that you constantly need "improvement" to be okay. Whether that form of betterment is looking younger, thinner, more muscular, less hairy, or whatever, believe me, it's not real. Buying products won't save you! Helping others and having more human connections will.

CHAPTER 5 WRAP-UP

UNFOLLOW ACCOUNTS THAT MAKE YOU FEEL BAD ABOUT YOURSELF. INSTEAD, PROMOTE ACCOUNTS—INCLUDING YOUR OWN—THAT CELEBRATE DIVERSE BODIES.

DATE PEOPLE FROM ALL BODY TYPES; CHALLENGE YOUR SEXUAL IDEAL.

STOP TALKING ABOUT EATING HEALTHY ALL THE TIME.

REJECT THE "FITNESS" UNIVERSE.

GROW YOUR MIND INSTEAD OF FOCUSING ON THE SUPERFICIAL.

6

TOXIC MONOGAMY

The title of this chapter may be deceiving. Monogamy isn't wrong or bad; if that's the kind of love you're looking for, fine! But the way we've been taught to run our relationships—the dominant, traditional relationship model—*is* toxic, because it's based on capitalist norms that don't serve us. That narrative prioritizes competition over love or generosity, even within a relationship. This plays out in multiple ways, including the tired trope that women need to compete with each other to "get a man," the idea that people can be happy only in a committed relationship, and the idea that if someone is single they must be "too picky," repressed, shutdown, or doing something wrong.

This also manifests in the idea that a relationship is little more than a race to an engagement ring. But who says? Love is so much bigger than the tedious, one-note story we've been spoon-fed all our lives. Love shouldn't be based on deprivation or centered on ownership ("put a ring on it"). Success in relationships is about transformation, health, love, and enrichment, not finances, objects (houses or cars), or relationship duration. Partners don't "possess" each other—not their bodies, not their time, not their fantasies, or anything else. True partnership is about sharing, *not* owning.

Grow sideways.

The old, broken relationship trajectory claims that "growing up" and reaching adulthood means falling in love, getting hitched, having kids, and living out a perfectly curated (and, some would argue, perfectly boring) life of traditional gender roles and age-based norms. But who says when "adulthood" happens and what it means to every individual? Personally, I don't believe in growing up; I believe in growing sideways. This means expanding beyond the world's arbitrary, oppressive rules into self-defined rules that feel right *to you.*

To grow "sideways" instead of "up" is to ignore the social constraints for each chronological stage—especially within sex and relationships. Psychology and general culture have an obsession with psychosocial "stages of development" that carry an inherent sense of criticism: if you're forty and single, there's something wrong with you. If you never get married, you're a weirdo. If you don't want kids, you're selfish or missing out. If you don't have a nine-to-five corporate job, you're a slacker. There's no room in that limited view of "adulthood" for true growth or individuality. It's stifling, and it prevents people from tapping in to the kind of life they authentically want. Maybe, for you, adulthood isn't centered on ageist expectations. Maybe you don't want the house, or the kids, or the husband/wife/picket fence/whatever. That's fine! Our culture is fixated on family, but having a family in the hypertraditional sense is not for everyone. Though I'm obviously a proponent of relationships, I'm an even bigger proponent of being true to yourself and following your authentic dreams, whatever those look like for you.

Maybe in your version of adulthood you'll opt to prioritize your career, or leisure, or travel, or entertainment; maybe relationships and family are secondary or don't come into play at all. Maybe your family is made up of your friendships, your pets, or your volunteer work. Our standard relationship models often don't work, and we need to create new ones—not simply continue to lock ourselves in flawed cycles.

Dear Dr. Chris,

I'm a thirty-year-old man. I'm bisexual, though I rarely get into relationships with men; I'll have sexual flings with them, but I'm more romantically geared toward relationships with women. I recently started dating a woman who jokingly mentioned, on our first date, that she wouldn't date a man who had slept with another guy. I was hurt and offended, but I clammed up and felt I couldn't tell her the truth. I really like her and I'm upset that this might be a deal breaker. Is there any way to help her come around?

DR. CHRIS: Many people feel more strongly drawn romantically to one gender and more sexually attracted to another gender. I understand how blindsiding that moment must have felt for you; I also understand why your first instinct was to shut down and stay silent. But now that you've had some time to consider this woman's comment from all sides, let's evaluate it a little more clearly. Her struggle to understand bisexuality reveals a common insecurity about the idea that one can be attracted to multiple genders. Society has taught us that someone who has been with a man once (or more) can't be into women as well.

Love isn't a competition, so this woman shouldn't be internally competing with other men (or women) for your affections. She may have internalized the belief that man-on-man sex is somehow "dirtier" or riskier than sex between men and women, which is absolutely untrue. In any case, you need to tell her the truth. Make this a teachable moment in which you practice authenticity, both to build intimacy and assess compatibility. It's possible that her eyes can be opened to different types of sexuality outside her norm and that she can develop confidence in your ability to be with her in the ways she wants relationally and sexually. And if she is still disgusted, doesn't understand, and is not willing to listen or learn? Then it's probably time to stop dating her.

If you're in a monogamous relationship—or you want to be—but don't understand why you're still unhappy, unfulfilled, or unsettled, take heart. One of the reasons so many monogamous relationships fail is because most of us *don't know how to have them.* There's a super-high divorce rate not because people love monogamy and are doing it right but because so many of us are doing it wrong. If we start viewing monogamy in a healthier way, instead of linking it so closely to toxic mores that seep into our psyches from mass culture, our relationships can last longer—and be far happier.

If you want healthy relationships, you have to break the rules (I'll keep reminding you of that, over and over, until it registers!). This chapter will explain how. I'll tell you what the old guard wants you to do and what I want you to do. If you're looking for a genuine, happy relationship—monogamous or not—I suggest you ditch the outdated advice and follow my guidelines instead.

Don't compete. Do see yourselves as a team.

I see a lot of clients in relationships who act as if they're actually in competition with their partners. They'll come into my office for couples therapy and look at each other like "it's you versus me." But you absolutely cannot have a healthy, sustainable relationship with that mind-set. Love is not a game, a fight, a competition, or a battlefield, no matter what the songs say. You're teammates, not opponents. Your partner shouldn't be judging you, assessing you, or trying to outshine or one-up you. I teach these patients to reframe their attitude about relationships from "me" and "I" to "we" and "us" and to start thinking like a team and a couple; they're in it together.

Don't seek "fairness." Seek mutuality.

So many people have this false idea that life and relationships are supposed to be fair, just, and equitable. Sure, it would be great if that were true, but that's a fantasy world; relationships are all about mutuality. Maybe one of you agrees that cleaning is your thing and the other focuses on taking care of the pets. When relationships are mutual, there's mutual power. All partners have the ability to influence each other.

Don't idolize individualism or avoid enmeshment. Embrace an "us/we" mentality instead of an "I/you" mind-set.
Codependence has an incredibly bad rap in our society and in the world of psychology, but that rap is unfounded. Despite our culture's fixation on monogamy, the idea of "needing" one's partner is often stigmatized, mocked, and turned into twelve-step fodder instead of being embraced. But healthy relationships are actually all about fusion and healthy enmeshment. Depend deeply on each other—it's okay! In fact, I don't really believe in codependence being problematic at all.

I know a couple is healthy if they come into my office talking about "we" and "us"—"what we want" and "what *we're* doing" instead of "what I need" and "what *I* want to do." Of course, our culture seems A-OK with hyperdependence on career, technology, and machines, but when it comes to relying on people or actually needing others, we're trained to shame or pathologize it. We need to rely more on others and less on technology and move away from this sense that individualism and separation are more noble than connection and dependence. We shouldn't be running our relationships like a business! That kind of narcissistic, "what's in it for me?" mentality doesn't serve us when it comes to forming and sustaining healthy relationships. Business may be a competition, but love is not.

Don't enter relationships with a goal in mind (marriage, kids, status)—enter them for the potential of love and transformation.

Relationship "success" isn't determined by meeting an arbitrary goal like getting engaged, getting married, or having kids. (Nothing wrong with wanting kids, of course, but relationships can't promise this from the start.) Instead, you should be entering relationships in search of transformation and love, not in the hopes of gaining financial support or social status. (I know those ideas are drilled into our heads from an early age, though, especially for women.)

Remember, relationships of any length are supposed to change you! There's nothing wrong with being single, but I also believe that we do our best growing when we're in relationships. Every movie is about relationships, every song is about relationships, and every book is about relationships, so many of us spend much of our lives seeking them out. We should be trying to do relational work if that's what our goal is. If your goal isn't to be single, then don't "practice" learning how to be single; that's not a worthy goal.

Seek relationships to expand your life: to help you grow and shift. They're intended to disrupt you in important and crucial ways. If your standard schedule and daily life aren't being shaken up by a partner, someone is selling out their authenticity for comfort. And remember, there's no such thing as relationship stability; things can and will change. Just because today you think you want to be with someone "forever" does not mean you'll be on the same page next year. I love being in a relationship and when I'm single I can't wait to be in another committed one. Hence, I never want to get too comfortable on my own, because staying single is not a long-term goal of mine. When I'm not dating anyone I'm still practicing being relational with my friends and sex partners, reading books about healthy relationships, and thinking in those terms about the world.

CLIENT CASE STUDY

A few years back, two men came to me extremely frustrated by their inability to adopt a child. "Rob" and "Trevon" had been trying to adopt for years but kept coming up against all kinds of painful and discriminatory hurdles. Both men had subscribed to the idea that having kids would somehow legitimize their relationship, that it was the "next step" in a happy and idyllic domestic life, but it was unclear to me whether either of them deeply wanted kids for the sake of the children themselves: to help children grow up, teach them, love them, and help mold them. Rob and Trevon were also surrounded by friends who had families of multiple children, and they found themselves in a constant dance of comparison and despair about what they didn't have yet.

I reminded them that there *really are no rules*, that each relationship is unique. There is no right way or wrong way to live or to be in a relationship. I helped them discover, together, what "us" and "we" meant to them and to evaluate their own true wants and needs instead of comparing themselves to their friends. After various sessions and lots of discussion about their dreams and goals, they became recommitted to their goal of adopting—but this time it was for the right reasons.

Don't use timelines to determine a relationship's success. See each relationship as a stand-alone entity with its own unique value.

The success of a relationship isn't based on how long it lasted. A relationship can be powerfully transformative yet last only a day, a week, or a month. In fact, lots of—if not most!—healthy, strong relationships don't last forever, and we need to get rid of the idea that only long-term partnerships have meaning. If you met someone interesting, grew as a person, and had a great time (or a mostly great time) in the process, you should consider your relationship a resounding success. Ask yourself, "Was I a good partner and did I grow?" rather than, "How long were we together?" as a way to gauge this.

Don't ever act like you "own" your partner. You're individuals with your own hopes, goals, and sexualities.

No one belongs to you. "My husband," "my girlfriend," "my partner," "my spouse": these kinds of expressions are about ego and anxiety, not love. When you fear losing someone, you try to control them and make them "yours." But no one is truly yours, and we need to let go of this way of thinking. If you put someone in a prison, don't act surprised when they try to escape! Also let go of the idea that you have any say or input over your partner's sexual fantasies and turn-ons. You don't. Your goal should be to care for them and help foster their growth as a person. Out of anxiety and attempts to control, many people actually limit their partners' growth because it scares them. But this is not what love is. Give your loved ones the freedom and care to be wholly themselves—even if that means you're a little uncomfortable sometimes.

Don't look for perfection. Allow "good enough" to exist in your relationships.

Nothing and no one is perfect. There's no such thing. We all know this on a logical level, but when it comes to understanding it emotionally, many of us start to falter. We keep secretly believing or hoping that perfection will arrive in the form of a partner or a relationship. We assume that with the "right one," our relationships will flow like magic, that there will be no hiccups, hardships, or bumps in the road. But this is nothing more than fantasy! There's no "right one," and there's no perfect. Every human we're engaging with—whether they're a long-term partner or a stranger on the street—carries their own baggage, their own flaws, and their own internal struggles. All these things manifest in our relationships. Don't expect things to be effortless in a relationship. Love takes work; things can get hard; obstacles will arise. It's all a part of what makes it so rich and so worth it in the end.

Don't subscribe to the idea that there are always only two options: in or out, broken up or together, single or partnered.

There are way more possibilities when it comes to our relationships than most of us realize, and we should be creating these possibilities for ourselves. Things don't have to be all or nothing, black or white. There are countless shades of gray. Even if a relationship changes course, you don't have to end things forever or cut anyone out of your life completely. When healthy relationships end, it happens in a loving way and your ex can and should stay in your life in some fashion. It may no longer be a sexual or romantic thing, but maybe your ex can remain a friend so you'll still have access to some parts of them. If you're both into it (and single or nonmonogamous), you can also be sexual with them sometimes.

Sex with exes doesn't have to be a big deal *or* a deal breaker! All parties get to choose whatever level of interest, intimacy, or commitment they want to maintain with someone, but it doesn't have to be black or white, together or not, hate or love. Of course, sometimes they may want different things, in which case discussion and negotiation (or ending the relationship completely) might be appropriate.

SEXUAL DYSFUNCTION OR SEXUAL CONFUSION?

The bulk of "sexual dysfunctions" that appear in my office are far from being actual dysfunctions; they are *sexual confusions*. Remember, normal is not the goal when it comes to sex, yet so many of us find ourselves trapped under the weight of societal expectation regarding what a "normal" penis or vagina does or looks like.

From birth, our culture presents a very small range of practices and appearances as "normal" when it comes to healthy sexual functioning. But of course, we're all different, so each and every individual on the planet will operate differently sexually. Variations and hiccups are to be expected, and we will all have sexual snags at points in our lives. This is not pathology. This is not dysfunction. This is human sexuality. Most of what professionals deem "dysfunctions" are due not to disorder, or the failure of a particular part of the body, but rather to failure to perform sex in a way that is socially acceptable.

The problem is the paradigm, not the genitals. Sex is about far more than just how firm a penis is, how long it can stay that way, and how smoothly a vagina accepts penetration. Surgery or pills to solve "problems" ignore couples' issues, sexual interests, and intrapersonal struggles. Still, pharmaceutical companies and doctors have turned natural variations in sexual functioning into a biological problem to fix, either with medication or with flawed theories.

Our problematic obsession with "railing" (hard repeated thrusting), erections, penetration, and cumming (just like in the movies!) is making people confused and dissatisfied. Pleasure, not procreation, is the main goal of sex for most people. Erections and vaginal penetration are not required.

We are in a postgenital phase and must move the focus to other body parts. What to do?

- **LEAVE YOUR PENIS ALONE!** It's not meant to perform on demand. Constantly expecting your—or your partner's— penis to get hard and stay hard or reach orgasm isn't sex; it's show. This kind of pressure can lead to bad sex, not to mention long-term constriction and tension in the genitals and pelvic floor. It also reduces pleasure, which is obviously a primary goal for many of us when it comes to sex. Instead of getting sucked into this performance-driven trap of *doing*, focus on yourself: how sex *feels*.

- **STOP FOCUSING ON YOUR EXTERNAL PARTS.** We have dissociated, disembodied sex when we focus only on our external bodies during the act. Penis owners might find themselves worrying about their erections: how easy (or difficult) they are to get or maintain and how readily the penis ejaculates. But remember, you can orgasm without an erection ("soft penis" orgasm) and without penile stimulation. People with vaginas might fret about how their vaginas look, smell, or feel to their partners. Instead of this preoccupation with how your body looks, focus instead on how you feel—on the physical and emotional sensations you're experiencing.

- **RECOGNIZE DIFFICULTIES IN SEXUAL FUNCTIONING NOT AS "PROBLEMS" BUT AS CHALLENGES.** Facing these sorts of hurdles can ultimately be a good thing; they can help expand your understanding of how to be sexual and motivate you to experiment with things you've never tried.

- **THINK ABOUT THE FULL PICTURE.** Is the sex hot? Are you attracted to your partner? Is monogamy sucking your sexual soul? Do you need more diversity, or do you need to be single? Are you asking for what you want? If you're facing a sexual issue, don't ignore the possible underlying cause.

SEX WITH AN EX: WHEN IS IT OKAY?

When we start dating someone new, we might slowly work our way into their lives. But when we go through a breakup, we often try to rip ourselves out of their lives completely, even though this can sometimes create even more pain.

If you don't trust your ex or if they are abusive, you should absolutely terminate the relationship. If you feel utterly miserable and psychologically unable to get over an ex, you also might want to take enough space to allow yourself to heal before communicating with or seeing them again.

But if you had a healthy relationship in which one or both of you realized you simply weren't suited for a long-term relationship, you might want to consider remaining in each other's lives in some way.

Sex with an ex can be a soothing way to slowly work your way out of a relational commitment and to lovingly turn to each other for support as you learn to fly solo. The aim in this isn't to "get over" someone; it's to learn how to have them in your life in a different way. It's a good sign when you are friends with your exes because it means you don't burn things down as you leave commitments. It also leaves room to establish a new ongoing relationship with your ex.

Having "ex sex" also allows you to reenter the dating world still feeling datable and desirable, which isn't always the case in a nasty, painful breakup. The comfort of this type of sex provides a valuable bridge back out into singledom, while allowing you to keep each other company and enjoy some of what brought you together.

Work toward evolving relationships that can continue with some sort of sex or friendship when exclusivity or romance ends. This is one of the many gifts brought on by dating with compassion.

Don't buy into the idea that if you're in love, your partner won't be attracted to anyone else. Remember that just because they're your partner doesn't mean they're not human.

Believing that if you're in love, your partner will never be attracted to anyone else is, well, straight-up delusional. Sorry, but we're just not wired that way, whether we're in love or not. Your sexual instincts will always be ignited by seeing someone you find sexy or attractive, and that's perfectly acceptable. (But maybe your partner doesn't want to hear about it, which is also normal.)

So many of us mistakenly treat our partners like they're a car: it's my car; I own it; no one else should drive it; I get to decide who gets in and out of it and where it's parked. But as we've established earlier, people aren't possessions. The ownership model is problematic because it leads to destructive lines of thinking: "You're mine now and I don't want to share you; I'm threatened by the idea of your having a connection with anyone who isn't me; I can't handle knowing that you might find another person attractive in the world." These ways of thinking are self-centered and destructive. This is another moment when you must practice trust. And again, if trust is not there, that's your biggest issue to resolve—not whether or not your partners find others attractive (which, of course, they do).

THE "BEST FRIEND" MYTH

I believe healthy dependence is a great thing, but that manifests differently for different relationships. Not everyone desires an intense, emotional reliance on their partner, and that's perfectly fine. People shouldn't go into relationships thinking their partner can or should meet their every single need in life. Another healthy relationship model is a community or a social-based system in which your friends can fill in the gaps for whatever your partner doesn't bring to the table. For some people, a romantic partner is mainly there for romance and sexuality, not for friendship or social support. Romantic love isn't the be-all and end-all for everyone. Most of us aren't going to get all our needs—intellectual, psychological, sexual—met by one person, and that's okay. I personally tend not to date people who are too academic or intellectual; I save that stuff for my friends, whom I spend hours of my downtime with, geeking out, debating, and philosophizing. When I come home, I prefer to do other things with the people I date (as well as being sexual and affectionate with them, of course).

Don't get angry if your partner is friends with exes (or is friends with people of whatever gender they're attracted to). Remember, you don't own each other.

Again we see that ownership-based capitalist model of "you're mine; I own you now." Nope, love is about transformation and learning how to allow your partner to have other relationships in their life. When we get into a relationship, our world should get bigger, not smaller; we shouldn't *lose* people! We should be adding our partner's friends and family to our world, letting things become more expansive. You should never have to get rid of your exes just because you're seeing someone who isn't secure enough to accept those friendships.

Some intimacy-phobic experts call these kinds of friendships "emotional cheating" and shame deep friendships or multiple forms of intimacy with others. These types of relationships are actually healthy, though, and you should support this in your partner's life. The guideline is that *any friend who is a friend of your relationship gets to stay.* This means exes or friends who support your relationship and do not try to do or say things that disrespect it should be allowed to remain in your life. One caveat: good friends will always tell you if they are concerned about your relationship for a legitimate reason—for instance, if they notice warning signs that your partner is controlling or abusive. This is still being a "friend of your relationship."

Don't assume that your partner will never make you upset or provoke disappointment, hurt, or discomfort. Accept that growth involves discomfort.

Healthy relationships are about intimacy, and intimacy can be scary. It can be hard. It can trigger fear, anxiety, and discomfort. Don't buy into the idea that love is supposed to be simple, carefree sailing at all times. If you're nervous before talking to your partner about something, acknowledge it and then embrace it. That sense of unease means you're bringing up something powerful and important to you; it's an opportunity for growth as a person and as a couple. Superficial intimacy (sharing only surface-level conversations) is not real intimacy. Real intimacy is admitting, "I'm anxious about saying this and it might make you nervous to hear it, but I want to be known, and I want to know you." Even if your partner comes to you with something that triggers fear, anxiety, or discomfort (they aren't happy with your sex life, want to open up the relationship, want to take a break, or whatever), try to hear them and appreciate what they've told you. Your job in a healthy relationship is to be known deeply, to be transformed—and you can do this only if you're being authentic.

CHAPTER 6 WRAP-UP

HEALTHY RELATIONSHIPS OFTEN INVOLVE SOME FORM OF EMOTIONAL DEPENDENCE. THERE'S NOTHING WRONG WITH NEEDING OTHERS.

A RELATIONSHIP'S SUCCESS CAN'T BE GAUGED BY HOW LONG IT LASTS. NOT ALL GREAT RELATIONSHIPS LAST FOREVER, BUT THAT DOESN'T MEAN THEY "FAILED."

EMBRACE "WE" INSTEAD OF "ME."

BEING FRIENDS WITH EXES IS A HEALTHY THING; DON'T GET PISSED AT YOUR PARTNER FOR BEING FRIENDS WITH AN EX.

YOU AND YOUR PARTNER DON'T OWN EACH OTHER IN ANY WAY, SHAPE, OR FORM—EVEN IF YOU "PUT A RING ON IT."

IF YOU'RE IN A RELATIONSHIP, YOU AND YOUR PARTNER ARE BOTH GOING TO GET HURT AT SOME POINT. THIS IS NATURAL AND HEALTHY; DISCOMFORT BRINGS GROWTH.

WORK LESS, DATE MORE

We need love, touch, intimacy, and close connections with other people now more than ever. Of course, many of us forget this, especially in today's frenetic times. Some of my clients work like machines and prioritize their jobs over their relationships and families. They come to see me with a vague hope of getting "fixed" and "healed"— not because they crave more intimacy or happier relationships but because they want to return to work and be "productive" enough to get back out there and achieve more superficial signs of status. It's a toxic cycle that won't make you happier in the long run.

Why? Because it's been proven that relationships, not work, status, or money, provide lasting happiness and serenity. All the shit people blindly seek out in drugs, crappy food, and consumerism can be found in love, sex, and attachments: oxytocin, comfort, connection, intimacy. The brain is a social organ. It's built on relationships and maintained by relationships. None of these things are available in replacement forms. Intimacy, in the interpersonal and neurobiological sense, requires intentional touch, time together, and eye contact, three things that sadly can't be bottled, packaged, or dosed out— even by me.

Work Narcissism

In my office, I hear it all the time. Client after client comes in complaining that their relationships or their health is tanking because of their work. But instead of unpacking this and vowing to change it, they just roll over and accept it. They don't question their own priorities; they don't pause for even a moment. They won't push themselves on it, so I have to remind them: when your primary life goals are work, finances, and career at the expense of relationships, yep, your intimate relationships *will* suffer.

Why are we allowing our work to come before our human connections, and more importantly, why would we ever think that kind of lifestyle would make us happy? It's nothing more than work narcissism; it's putting business values before relational human values, and no one thinks there's a problem with that?

Children who don't have a strong primary attachment early in life—which is also tied to physical touch, by the way—often don't thrive. They can develop psychological, physical, and emotional problems that last a lifetime. Why do I mention this? To prove my point that relationships and human contact are the most nourishing, important things we can have. And those relationships certainly don't have to be romantic or sexual to qualify. I'm talking about friendship. I'm talking about fuck buddies. I'm talking about someone you hug hello when you see them. I'm talking about family members you can call and pour your heart out to.

We have so many forms of relationships in our lives and there doesn't need to be a hierarchy. Whether it's my best friend, my mom, or the neighbor I smile at every day, these human connections are actively nourishing both my brain and my heart. Sorry, but work simply can't do that. Work pays the bills. It might also give you an ego boost; socially, you've been trained to believe that power and status reign. Our identities may *feel* tied to jobs, money, and status, but that's a social construct. It's false and it's fragile.

People get fired. People lose their jobs. People retire. You can't depend on work to sustain you in any meaningful way beyond your bank account.

You Are Not Your Job

I get it—most of us *have to* work. It's a sad truth in a capitalist society: we work to support ourselves and our families. The problem occurs when our identities become so tied up with our jobs that we can't find self-esteem without work. But a fancy job won't keep you warm at night. What matters is making enough money to get by at a job you don't hate that, hopefully, gives you sufficient free time to see friends and family, have sex, travel, and do whatever leisure activities you're into. A summer house and a statusy job won't promise or deliver anything substantial or life-affirming. They certainly can't promise happiness, but improving your relationships *can*.

To clarify: it's great if you love your job. If you've managed to build a career that feels personally fulfilling to you *and* pays your rent, that's amazing—congratulations. Finding true meaning in their work is, for most people, quite challenging, if not impossible. That's why I de-emphasize work as a source of meaning or identity to begin with. We put too much pressure on ourselves to love our jobs or to "do what we love." That advice looks great on a Hallmark card or an inspirational meme, but it ignores the massive systems of oppression and poverty that fuel this nation.

Most Americans literally can't afford (or aren't supported) to "do what they love" or even to take the time to sit around pondering what that might be. Which is also part of why I think we need to start de-emphasizing work as a culture. Work to live; don't live to work. If you've known since you were a kid that you wanted to pursue writing and you managed to make that happen—that is, you some-how stumbled upon all the necessary financial, social, and personal resources to do that—good on you. Most people don't have those privileges. Most people take jobs they're "meh" about because they need money. Which is perfectly okay—great, even. What's not great is when people work themselves into the ground and ignore their need for companionship, passion, and love solely to feed their egos and make themselves feel important.

I didn't always feel this way, by the way. I always had high ambitions for myself, and I wanted a career that would pay my bills while it also helped people tap into their truest, most authentic selves. The more feminist and social justice training and socialization I received, the more I began focusing my practice—and my life!—on community, cooperation, and relationality. Internalizing those feminist, relational-based therapy models started to help me recognize all the ways I need to help my clients (and my readers) challenge both consumerism and workaholism, because they're two parts of the same puzzle—and both are deadening our capacities for healthy relationships.

Another thing I noticed was just how slight of a sense many of my clients had of their real selves. For instance, when I asked certain clients, "What do you like to do for fun, leisure, or pleasure?" they didn't know how to answer. They'd never been given permission to have fun or seek pleasure because they'd bought into society's focus on work above all, on work *becoming who you are.*

But rarely are we given the support or encouragement to just do something fun, simply for the sake of pleasure or connection. A lot of traditionally socialized men are so accustomed to being steered away from relationships and toward their professions that they think showing up every now and then for their child or their partner should get them a gold star. They think cooking dinner, picking up the kid, or helping the baby get dressed in the morning makes them Dad of the Year. Hell, no—sorry dude, but that's not good enough. We need more consistent examples of support and positive relationality than that.

WHAT'S EMOTIONAL LABOR?

Emotional labor has become a bit of a buzzword in the past few years, but its meaning couldn't be more straightforward. In essence, it's the work someone does in managing a relationship or doing the emotional work of a relationship. Women are generally tasked with doing more of the emotional labor in their relationships due to the way women are socialized in our culture—to initiate conversations, deal with scheduling, set up appointments, manage the inner workings of their households, and listen to family concerns. While this emotional type of work is different from other kinds of physical work, it's still *work*. It's not fun to juggle five hundred emotional tasks, relationships, and priorities in the air at all times, yet most women find themselves forced to do this. Note to the partners of these women: step up! Everyone has a part in fair and equal emotional labor. If you notice your partner taking on all the tasks of dealing with everyone's feelings and intimacy as well as running your family, or even your romantic relationship, jump in and help. Open up, express your feelings more, and even offer to do more chores; take the kids to practice, plan your vacations, whatever. And don't assume that your mere presence—or your financial support—gets you off the hook. It doesn't.

CLIENT CASE STUDY

A couple whom I'll call "Tom" and "Jill" once came in to see me. Tom was frustrated that Jill had taken an extremely time-consuming new job and appeared to be prioritizing work over him. He complained that he didn't feel close or connected with her anymore. He felt that her job had become her life, and he was worried about the fate of their relationship because of this.

One issue for Tom was that when Jill got home from work—Tom was a stay-at-home dad and took care of their two kids—she wouldn't make time to totally disconnect from the office. She continued to check her phone during dinner, e-mail during TV shows, and finish up paperwork, sometimes even in bed. Her attempts to multitask were severely damaging their relationship, but she was just too distracted to see it.

When Tom told me this (in front of Jill), she was shocked by how unhappy he was. She hadn't even realized the extent of their disconnection or how badly it bothered him.

I told them that transitions are important, and when Jill comes home, she needs to acknowledge her partner. The first thing she should do is touch Tom—hold him, kiss him, hug him. There should be some kind of welcome-home ritual that helps boost the relationship. And then if she absolutely has to continue doing any work, she should do it later in the evening.

I also told them to enforce a "no work in the bedroom" rule. They needed to leave phones outside, leave laptops in the living room, and leave all paperwork elsewhere. Their bedroom needed to become their private couple zone: their place to unwind, cuddle, connect, and have sex.

Tom and Jill managed to make some adjustments and keep their relationship alive, but that's not always the case. I've worked with couples whom I had to tell bluntly that they had to choose love or career, because there clearly wasn't room for both.

The Productivity Trap

American culture's obsession with productivity is evident in pretty much everything we do, from our predilection to working long hours to our obsessive devotion to our smartphones. Because our work lives no longer end when we're off the clock (what does "off the clock" even mean these days?), we rely on tech for nearly everything: to balance our bank accounts, meditate, make lists, take notes, set timers, track our fertility, remind ourselves to have sex(!), and unplug from the Internet. Constantly fixated on multitasking, we use apps instead of learning to set good boundaries for our work lives *or* our home lives; in fact, most of us have no balance between the two at all. (Balance would be the minimal goal, by the way: our relationships should ideally receive the most attention and energy.) We check our e-mails at the dinner table; we're on social media before we've even gotten out of bed in the morning. We're sleeping less and dying more suddenly due to stress.

Addiction and depression are the "canaries in the coal mine" of our times. I watch the deluge of antidepressant commercials, none of which are addressing what I believe to be the root cause of many of these conditions: lack of connection. Same for addiction treatment centers. All the solutions we keep pointing ourselves toward are Band-Aids that ignore the real, systemic causes of our ills.

Multitasking as a means to productivity isn't *actually productive*—and it just might be killing our relationships. Our brains can generally only handle doing one thing at a time. If you're constantly switching between tasks, your brain can't effectively focus on, well, anything. You may be doing something—writing a paper, say—but when you get pulled away to heed the siren call of checking Facebook, you're also simultaneously juggling the knowledge that you *should* be doing something else. Guilt creeps in as you procrastinate. You check Twitter. You look at your bank statement. You call your sister back. All these banal tasks prevent you from feeling at ease, because you're avoiding the important stuff and you're not legitimately accomplishing anything.

As you can imagine, this takes a huge toll on your relationships, too—you're never fully present or undistracted for your partner, your dates, or your sex life. Ever tried multitasking on a date? It doesn't go over too well. In fact, I believe that, barring an emergency, people should put their phones away entirely when they're out with significant others. Sorry kids, but your phone doesn't belong on a restaurant table.

More Touch = More Happiness

One of the biggest things our culture's hyperfocus on work does is starve us of touch and affection. The drive for physical comfort via skin-on-skin contact is one of the most primal, powerful drives we have—far stronger than the urge to work, consume, or be "productive." Remember that 1950s study in which monkeys chose fluffy fake "mother" monkeys that didn't have milk over cold, unfuzzy wire "mothers" that did provide milk? That says something about humans, too (hey, monkeys are practically our brothers, okay?).

In essence, humans actually *need* physical connection to be happy and feel secure, and most of us aren't getting nearly enough human contact on any level, physical *or* emotional. (One out of four Americans says they have *no one* to talk with about important issues—alarming, right?)

A warm touch like a hug or a kiss (or a good roll in the sack) triggers the production of oxytocin, also known as the bonding hormone. As a neurochemical, oxytocin has been proven to lower stress and anxiety; it also promotes feelings of trust and safety. Not getting enough oxytocin—or enough physical touch in general—can contribute to depression, anxiety, and other mood disorders, as well as increase one's propensity for loneliness. Over the last few years, researchers have learned that more and more of us are growing lonelier and lonelier, and this sense of social isolation can be life-threatening: it compromises immune function and can trigger inflammation in the body. It's also about as deadly as smoking.

All of this is to say that most of humankind is literally starving for more touch and tactile communication: hugging, sex, massage, kissing, hand-holding. We need to stop ignoring the needs of our physical bodies, our need for connection. One great way to connect is, obviously, sex. Most people still don't see sex as a legitimate form of intimacy or as a valid way to "get to know someone." Many therapists and doctors (with the exception of me, of course) don't prescribe it as a healing intervention, and that's a mistake. Sex can be as useful as massage therapy when it comes to healing people's bodies and souls.

You have your priorities backward if you're prioritizing your job above your relationships. People psychologically and emotionally starve without love and touch—but there is no food bank for this. Our goal as human beings is to relate and love, not to work until we die.

When work-obsessed clients come in to see me, their "issues" tend to manifest in a few different ways. The first is that they're simply exhausted to the core. Like, really exhausted—too exhausted to put any energy into anything remotely sexual, relational, or, well, positive and life-affirming. If they're single, they don't date because they claim they're too wiped out. If they're partnered or married, they don't have sex because, again, they're too drained. Instead they come home from work, plop down in front of the TV, eat, drink beer or wine (if they're fancy), and watch Netflix for hours instead of actually speaking or holding their partner (or going out to meet a date). Their physical exhaustion may be real, but it's not something most of them have to accept—this is their fate only because they're choosing to make work a priority over their love lives. What does this mean? The short of it is that they're left with no love lives to speak of.

Another complaint? Some clients come to me claiming that they simply "don't have time" to engage in sex or a relationship. Translation: they're too busy with work. So many of them have either fading or nonexistent romantic and sexual lives because they haven't learned how to fold the erotic, the sexual, and the relational into their day-to-day work lives. Everyone can find ways to bring more of their erotic life into their work lives. On your break, you should be checking in with your loved ones—send loving, sexy texts and e-mails; surprise each other whenever you can. This might seem like a minor thing, but it goes a long way in preserving your connection to someone throughout the day.

Give Yourself Permission to Seek Pleasure

Most of us need to work to make ends meet financially, and I would never tell you to quit your job to stay home and cuddle. Classism and privilege come into play again here, and I'm well aware that most of us don't have sufficient financial resources to cut back our hours at work to pursue pleasure and leisure instead. We live in a practical world.

That said, we have a long way to go when it comes to allowing ourselves more fun, enjoyment, and meaning in our lives. We're pleasure phobic and leisure phobic. If someone came up to you and announced that they work twenty hours a week and they devote the other twenty hours to, say, surfing, or pottery, or traveling, or sex, you'd probably raise an eyebrow and say, "Who do they think they are? How selfish! So lazy! They must be independently wealthy! Or a spoiled brat!"

I get it. But in my book, people like that should actually be applauded. Because if you have the means to bring more playtime into your life—whatever that looks like for you—please do it. When you're on your deathbed, you won't regret not working more. You'll regret not telling people you loved them, not traveling with your partner(s), not indulging your passions, and not doing the things you loved and having more adventures.

How can you do these things if you're one of the gazillions of people with a long-ass day job and not enough time for extraneous fun? Again, work leisure and romance into your life in small doses however you can. If you're partnered, send your lover flirty texts throughout the day. On your days off, make sure to do things that enhance your life in a deeper way—don't just sit around watching TV (I mean, that's fine to do sometimes, but try to do other stuff, too). Use your free time to enhance your life on a deeper level, whether that's taking a course, reading a book, going on a date, or going to the beach to commune with nature. Do the things that make you feel good. Commit yourself to growth, personal expansion, and spending quality time with the people who matter most to you.

Relational Esteem > Self-Esteem

Self-esteem is fundamentally important. Crucial, even. I want everyone to walk through the world feeling amazing about themselves: like the hottest, realest, truest version of themselves. I want everyone to believe in their best self and to know that their best self is possible without having to change a single thing about what they look like or who they are. True self-esteem can come only with genuine self-acceptance, which means *radical self-acceptance:* accepting every single part of you, "flaws" and all.

But while I support people's quests for self-love, I also don't believe self-esteem should be our top priority. Why? Because relational esteem is more important. Relational esteem is about what you give (it's others-focused), while self-esteem is about, well, you. Happiness isn't about self-help; it's about relational help. It's not about self-improvement; it's about relational improvement.

Relationships are the highest path to finding ourselves. Just like you can't find legit, bone-deep happiness from a book, you can't find self-knowledge or self-love there either. You *can* find happiness and self-love through loving others. You can find it through relating to people, bumping up against obstacles with them, navigating sticky conversations with them, learning not to abandon them when you get scared, and committing to sticking around and working on your insecurities with them. You can't truly know and love yourself until you've let someone know and love you. Plus, the way you relate to others is usually the way you relate to yourself, so if you're closed off and isolated from people, I'd wager that you're also shut off from yourself and, well, not necessarily thriving.

How to increase your relational esteem? It's actually pretty easy. You start putting your relationships first. If you're a loner type, this means you need to get out there and relate. Of course, I wouldn't advocate a personality transplant (not that it's even possible), but you'll need to commit to doing one thing each day that pushes you past your comfort zone when it comes to building or sustaining relationships. Maybe it's reaching out to an old acquaintance via e-mail, adding a new friend on Facebook, or smiling at a stranger on the street. Maybe it's taking a volunteer position at a soup kitchen or doing a community rebuilding project in an area that was hit by a natural disaster. Maybe it's joining a book club. Maybe it's going to an animal shelter, talking to the staff, and adopting a cat. Whatever it is, do it.

We can't truly find meaning in our lives without having people around us to support us and build us up.

Always Be "Relationshipping"

Americans love to extol the wonder of the work-life balance. The problem is, we have none. I'm a fan of reading, therapy, and relational improvement, which is clearly what I'm trying to orient people toward with this book. But instead of focusing on self-improvement or improving your "work-life balance," focus on bettering your relationships. Ask yourself, "Am I prioritizing my relationship? Am I giving it time and attention every day?"

Because relationships aren't something you get once and then your work is done. It's not like you flirt, you date, you get your partner, and then it's finito, box checked, you're good to go. Being in a relationship isn't a done deal that you check off a to-do list. It's an ongoing exchange. You're either relationshipping or you're not. So make sure you're always participating in growing and expanding your relationship—this means you're still flirting, you're still dating your partner, you're still trying to attract and eroticize them. You should be staying in that cycle for the entire duration of your relationship.

You can't just assume that your relationship will keep itself afloat without your active participation. Engage with your partner when you're away, even if it's just for the day—text them, e-mail them, call them, or FaceTime them.

We give yearly job reviews, but we don't check in with our partners about our relationship performance. We should be. Look at your own actions and behaviors in the context of your partnership, and keep reflecting on ways you can do better: "Am I putting enough time into it? Where can I improve? How supportive of a partner am I being on a day-to-day basis?" Check in every three or six months for "relationship reviews." Ask your partner, "What's it like being in a relationship with me? Are there any areas that you might lovingly and compassionately ask me to improve upon?"

Don't criticize your partner—make respectful, kind requests. For instance, don't say, "You never take out the garbage," or call them a jerk. Try something like "Hey, it would be really great if you would try to show me a little more affection or get more involved with tasks at home."

Dear Dr. Chris,

I'm in my late thirties. My parents were workaholics and perfectionists who told me that I should never settle for less than the best in literally anything. The way this panned out for me was an Ivy League education, multiple graduate degrees, and a new career as a doctor. I feel like I should be happy and fulfilled, but I'm not. Every day I wake up alone, feeling like I have nothing to show for my life other than my job. I'm not saying my work isn't great—it is. But I need more. What should I do?

DR. CHRIS: You should prioritize relationships in your life. Make that your new goal and the focus of your plans. You know the old adage "If you go out looking for a relationship, it won't happen"? Maybe it's true. Who knows? But you can certainly create the conditions for a relationship to take root—that's the goal. Go online! While I'm bored in line at Starbucks, I can also access people online that I wouldn't be bumping into otherwise. Another thing to do is live like you're single—because you are! I tell my patients this all the time. This means you have to do the work, so if you're at a coffee shop or a bookstore and someone makes eye contact, look back. You have to live single; be open and responsive. If someone smiles, smile back. If someone talks to you, keep the conversation going.

Another tip: if you want a relationship, get away from gender norms and values. Women need to do the flirting, too. If you want things, you have to be willing to be active. So ask someone out. Don't just make passive eye contact and let others approach you.

I once worked with a client who complained that guys never asked her out. She desperately wanted to be in a relationship. So I told her to first get rid of the gendered stereotypes and then create the conditions for a relationship to spring up. "Live single, and then take one more step," I told her. So here's what she did. One night she went to a restaurant to meet a girlfriend. On their way to their table, they passed a bar area where a guy was sitting by himself. He happened to look at her. She said to herself, "All right, I would normally just sit down. But Dr. Chris said to take one more step—a step I wouldn't normally take."

Nope, she didn't ask him out. You know what she did? She went to the bathroom. How does that lead to a date? you might be wondering. Because she had to walk by the bar to get to the bathroom, which gave them time to look at each other. She had to walk directly past him. On her way back to the table, he stopped her, and then they ended up talking and exchanging numbers because she took just one more step past her usual comfort zone.

CHAPTER 7 WRAP-UP

YOUR WORK IS NOT YOUR IDENTITY.

THERE'S A SERIOUS SHORTAGE WHEN IT COMES TO HUMAN TOUCH. FIND WAYS TO CONNECT THROUGH TOUCH, WHETHER THAT'S HUGS, KISSES, OR SEX.

LONELINESS IS AN EPIDEMIC; WE NEED TO FOCUS ON OUR HUMAN CONNECTIONS INSTEAD OF OUR JOBS.

HAVE "RELATIONSHIP REVIEWS" TO GO OVER THE STATE OF YOUR RELATIONSHIP WITH YOUR PARTNER. THESE ARE MORE IMPORTANT THAN YOUR JOB PERFORMANCE REVIEWS.

WORK-LIFE BALANCE IS A MYTH.

IF YOU WANT A RELATIONSHIP, CREATE THE RIGHT CONDITIONS FOR ONE.

YOUR BEST
SEX EVER

Traditional sex and dating rules are based on male (read: patriarchal and sexist) sexuality and are rooted in problematic values. Healthy sex and relationships require a whole new model that is divergent from standard and traditional sexual norms and ideals. What we call "normal" or "typical" sex is actually *male-centric* sex (goal-centered, penetrative, and orgasm based: get in and get off). A healthier model includes both partners' pleasure and is not centered on performance and the goals of penetration, erections, and orgasms. It's loud, sometimes messy, and not always done in positions that make our bodies look their "best." And most important, it focuses on the sex *you* most enjoy. Everyone orgasms if desired, but sometimes sex might only involve fingers or toys.

A lot of people reading this book will by now be familiar with my messages of sex positivity and inclusivity. But that doesn't mean everyone has figured out how to be a great partner, have a fun date, or have a mind-blowing sex life. This chapter is for you: the freaky masses who need help moving from ideology into action in the bedroom. Remember, most of us—about 95 percent—are "sexually creative" (aka kinky), while just a few of us primarily go for the traditional types of sex you see represented on TV and in other media.

In a sexually healthy and body-positive world, this chapter wouldn't be needed. But shame about who you are, how you look, and what turns you on absolutely exists, and we need to unlearn it if we want to have great sex. Most of us have been taught that sex should be something small and sanitized and private. But that's not conducive to healthy sex. This chapter is about allowing yourself to have sex the way nature intended it to be: big and loud and expansive and personal. Sex is about opening up, not shrinking down, and letting your body do weird things and make weird sounds. *Good sex is about letting it be messy.*

The Cultural Oppressors

These are the elements bred into us by a toxic culture that can make it challenging to relax, open up, and enjoy sex:

- **GENDER.** Limits what we see as sexual, what we allow to be sexual, and what parts of ourselves we see as sexual. Seeing sex acts and body parts in terms of "for men only" and "for women only" is destructive.
- **HETERONORMATIVITY (ALONG WITH ITS OFFSHOOTS TOXIC MASCULINITY, SEXISM, AND HOMOPHOBIA).** Restricts what's healthy or "normal" to hetero sex and presents marriage or monogamy as the ultimate goal for dating, love, or sex. This limits how we view sex, our partner choices, when and how we allow sex to occur, and the goals we set for sex.
- **SEX AND BODY SHAME.** Prevents us from asking for what we want and allowing our full bodies to be sexual; keeps us constricted and unrelaxed (relaxation is a prerequisite for full arousal).
- **GENITAL PRIVILEGE.** Limits sex to being exclusively about genitals and penetration.
- **SLUT-SHAMING.** Assumes those with many sex partners are not healthy, are not looking for love, are not able to commit, or are intimacy phobic.

SEX ASSESSMENT CHECKLIST

YOUR SEX LIFE MAY BE GETTING STAGNANT IF . . .

- Your sex life feels rote or routine.
- You don't feel comfortable talking about sex with your partner.
- You don't feel safe touching yourself or being open about your fantasies with your partner.
- You feel shame about your sexuality or body.
- You feel like you're often "up in your head" during sex.
- You're in a low-sex or no-sex relationship.
- You have anxiety about sex or during sex acts.
- You are unhappy with your erections or not orgasming.

YOU'LL BE HAVING THE GREAT SEX
YOU'RE AIMING FOR WHEN . . .

- Your whole body feels sexual.
- You know what arouses you and you ask for it.
- You are confident with or without having an erection.
- You feel comfortable with seeing your body as sexual.
- You can orgasm when you want to.
- You enjoy the sex you are having.
- You don't have shame about what arouses you or your body.
- Your sex life is creative and diverse.

Right off the bat, let's get one thing straight: the suggestions in this chapter may not apply for *absolutely everybody*. Nothing applies to everybody. Again, that's one of my biggest pet peeves about most sex books on the shelves: they try to universalize something that is incredibly individual. We're all different when it comes to what turns us on, how we like to be touched, what we fantasize about, and the kind of sex we want. It's not what you do but *how* you do it that matters. Relax, have no shame, and ask for what arouses you, while also being respectful of what your partner wants.

And the number-one thing to remember: great sex is about staying mindful and in the moment; it's about *being*, not *doing*. It focuses on the *inside* (how it feels), not the *outside* (how it looks, how it sounds, or what you are doing).

No Body Is the Same

One of the most crucial parts of having excellent sex is *asking lots of questions*. Never assume that everyone with a similar gender presentation or similarly gendered body is aroused in the same way. Not everyone is cis. Ask!

You need to ask because it's a turn-off when you talk about sucking someone's clit when they actually want you to suck their penis, or when you say you want to play with someone's breasts when they actually consider them their pecs. Not everyone "male presenting" wants "male" anatomical labels for their body, so you need to use and repeat the language your partner uses for their own body. Everyone has the right to name and define their anatomy and gender on their own terms.

Some vagina owners need oral sex to get off, while others need anal. Some like their clits played with, while others are too sensitive for direct stimulation. Some people with vulvas like a very gentle touch, and others respond best to deep pressure. This can change within each sex session depending on factors like someone's level of arousal, the time of the month, and the person's stage of life.

Some penis owners like nipple play or anal stimulation, and others don't. And there are plenty of other areas many of us tend to neglect or forget altogether. G-spot? How about the U-spot (bladder area), P-spot (perineum area), or the mouth of the cervix?

So consider what applies to you and work with it, and remember, not every woman wants to be thrown on a bed, held down, or spanked. Not every man identifies as dominant or a "top." Not every man has a penis; not every woman has a vagina. Some people have nonbiological penises like dildos and packers, and these are their genitals. Because we are all completely unique when it comes to our own genital structures, no sexual "move" will work on everyone or even feel comfortable for everyone. Don't mind-read. Ask and explore people's bodies individually, on a case by case basis. There is so much diversity in what makes us all sexually tick.

Start with a Massage

No matter what kind of sex you're having, starting sex with a massage is a great way to ease into the action and set your intentions. It's slow, it involves the full body, it's not directly linked to the genitals, and pleasure—not orgasm—is the goal.

Massage is purely about connection and enjoyment. It also builds body awareness, helps eroticize the entire body, helps you relax, and helps foster more closeness and intimacy. There's no wrong way to massage or be massaged; it's about feeling, not form.

ENGAGE IN FOREPLAY. We tend to think of foreplay as what a partner does to us, ignoring our own sexual bodies. Spend the day or hours before sex letting your arousal build: thinking, touching, and playing with yourself. Warm your body up. Let arousal build and carry it with you. Make some form of sexual contact with yourself first. *This reminds you to focus on yourself and how your body feels.* Connect with yourself before you connect with a partner.

DON'T LET SEX BE LINEAR. Sex should start off and finish in different ways. When you're having sex, get your energy going, build your arousal—and then just stay there. Don't rush off toward more stimulation or any goal of completion. Relax into and stay with the pleasure. Fast, hard sex makes the body and genitals tight, not relaxed. This tension isn't good consistently; it leads to less sensitivity, and then more sensation is needed. Practice having sex that is slow and allows for enjoying the subtle.

FOCUS ON BEING PRESENT, NOT ON HOW YOU LOOK. Stay in your body; don't overthink things, don't "perform," and don't objectify yourself. Your penis is not a dildo! Think in terms of how you *feel*, not what your body or your genitals look like. That is disembodied sex. It ignores how sex *feels* in favor of how sex looks or "should be." Remember, good sex focuses on the inside (how it feels), not the outside (how it looks, how it sounds, or what you're doing). Shame, anxiety, and stress actually restrict blood flow to the genitals and limit our ability to experience full arousal. It would behoove all of us to slow down, breathe, and get out of our heads and into our bodies while hooking up. This is your time to connect with yourself and your partner.

STAY CLOSE AFTER SEX. Remain close and touching your partner; try letting your genitals stay connected. How are you feeling after sex? Nourished, more alive, and happier? Or drained, flat, and down? Conventional sex (meaning performance- or penetration-based, outcome-driven sex) can do this sometimes. Regardless, let it all linger. Don't rush away. Sit and let yourself feel the subtle nuances of sensation and emotion that exist after sex. The transition out is as important as the transition in.

SELF-CARE AND HEALING HOMEWORK. Get regular full-body massages and engage in other forms of erotic touch, both alone or with someone else. If you don't currently have a partner, make a habit of touching, caressing, and massaging yourself. (See the next section for more tips on how to do this.)

GREAT SEX TIP

Try creating a fantasy or sexual curiosity checklist. This is exactly what it sounds like: a list of all the things that arouse you—sex acts, scenarios, objects, toys, places, people, ideas. Share it with your partner and discuss ways to incorporate those things into your sex life. No judging! You can also try creating a body map checklist, in which you use a picture of your body (or someone else's body!) and practice touching and sexualizing all the parts of it that appeal to you. (Remember to push yourself outside your comfort zone a bit. This is how you grow sexually and build more intimacy.) Show your partner exactly what you enjoy. And be sure to sexualize every part of your bodies—not just the genitals. Also, if you're in a relationship, be sure to eroticize your partner daily. Small and large acts of romance, affection, and eroticism (texts, touches, notes, looks, sexts, pic exchanges, flirtation, and, of course, sex) all keep your relationship sexual and help your partner associate you with arousal. If you want to maintain a long-term sexual partnership, this is vital. This also helps you be direct and specific about what you want sexually.

Masturbation: (Still) the Crown Jewel of Your Sexual Self

As I explained in Chapter 3, you cannot have a healthy, body-positive, sex-positive relationship with a partner if you don't have it with yourself first. I know this sounds cliché, but it's true.

Your whole body can and should be part of your sexual anatomy. Yet most of us—due to sex and body shame, skewed gender roles, toxic masculinity, and so on—tend to reduce what we see as our sexual selves to exclusively our genitals. Instead, we need to start seeing our *entire bodies* as sexual.

When you masturbate, try practicing pleasure without immediately going for your genitals. Use both hands to massage your body in other areas. Caress, rub, tickle, and recognize the ways that touching yourself can involve many parts of your body. This also trains you to be sexual with your partners in a way that involves the full body. It makes for all-around better sex!

Try starting a mindful masturbation practice. Commit to touching yourself daily for two weeks. Each day, spend at least fifteen minutes alone with yourself. Enjoy pleasing yourself in any way that feels right or exciting. Don't make orgasm the focus; just touch yourself for the sake of self-connecting. (If you get off, that's cool, too.)

Try some of these tips:

- Take masturbation as seriously as you do partnered sex.
- Set time aside for masturbation.
- Explore your entire body.
- Take breaks from using porn while masturbating (this helps you practice sexual mindfulness).
- Allow whatever thoughts or fantasies arise; they're all okay. This is not about judgment—it's about acceptance and celebration.
- Explore anatomy that sex-phobic culture tells you to avoid (like your anus, etc.).
- Engage in opposite-gendered play. (This means ignoring gender stereotypes—women can be tops; men can be bottoms. Strap it on, ladies, and bottom it up, guys!)
- Use toys—allow for new sensations and exploration.
- Allow *all* sounds, body movements, and fluids to flow.
- Don't necessarily seek orgasm, but if it happens, allow it. (Remember, arousal does not always have to end with an orgasm!)
- For people with a penis, this kind of play can be done with or without an erection. In general, sex, orgasm, and pleasure do not require an erection; all can be achieved with a soft penis.
- Again, stay in your body, not in your mind.

Even when it comes to our masturbation habits, we need to mix things up. Many of us turn to the same fantasies, memories, toys, and scenes over and over again. This starts getting overly formulaic and, well, boring. We start requiring those same patterns in order to reach orgasm—the same porn, or a certain level of intense physical stimulation, like only being able to orgasm with the Hitachi Magic Wand. We need to break out of these private sexual ruts and expand our own self-love practices. This will help make us better, more creative lovers and open the door for new, fun experiences with our partners.

Mind-Blowing Sex Doesn't Always Mean an Orgasm

We all have lots of work to do when it comes to unlearning what we've been taught about sex and our own pleasure. One of the biggest cultural myths that's kept many of us from having the kind of sex lives we want is the idea that sex is just about getting off. Yup, just as so many of us are obsessed with prioritizing work and status over relationships and pleasure, far too many of us are too focused on orgasm when it comes to sex. This might translate to thinking guys can't have fun if they're not fully hard or that sex is "pointless" if no one gets off.

Instead, we need to reframe the way we see sex, because *orgasm is not the goal!* Think about it—getting off does not inherently make sex "good." People have orgasms in all kinds of less-than-"good" situations, even with people they dislike, distrust, or are not attracted to. Orgasm can be an involuntary body response. Climax can be elusive or even impossible for some, even when someone is actively enjoying themselves in bed. We need to rid ourselves of the idea that simply *having an orgasm* makes sex worthwhile or "successful." Sex should be about fun, connection, play, and expansion.

Be Loud, Be Messy

We're socialized to be small and silent within our sexualities, but making sounds and letting our bodies get loud, messy, and even a little weird is empowering—and it's what healthy sex is all about. What we should be focusing on during sex is *pleasure for pleasure's sake*. Sexual intimacy is not as simple as getting off, getting your partner off, and calling it a day. The pursuit of true sexual enjoyment is wholly individual, which means you need to let yourself be open while you're doing it. Unapologetically go after what feels best to you; make noises, get wet, and let yourself experience unusual body movements—shaking, jerking, quivering, whatever. The energy created by moving around and making sounds also amps up your own arousal, keeping you more firmly in your body and in the experience. The goal for great sex should be "it feels good."

For Better Sex, Watch More (Ethical, Feminist, Female-Gaze) Porn—Together

As you know by now, I'm an advocate for porn. One way to help you connect with your partner—and learn about their unique turn-ons—is to ask them about the porn they watch. Ask them to describe the scenes they gravitate toward. Ask them to recount, in clear detail, exactly what they fantasize about. They could act it out, or even write a script or a recap of their fantasy. Then try watching them masturbate.

In the context of a relationship, if you're interested in watching porn with your partner but you feel shy about bringing it up, don't stress. Just take a breath and share the general themes in the porn you like to watch. Are they into it, too? If they don't have experience watching porn, ask what they think about while fantasizing, masturbating, or having sex. Next, you can go online together and start investigating some of the types of porn you're both into. While you're watching, check in with each other to see which parts are arousing and which ones aren't. (And if you're too busy doing, uh, other things, discuss it afterward!)

A caveat: In service of practicing slowing down and making sex about more than just orgasm, I recommend that people who always masturbate with porn also practice masturbating without it. This allows for more awareness of yourself and more mindful arousal. Solely masturbating with porn has caused some people to experience disconnection from their entire bodies and also to internalize the false perspective that sex is centered solely on release. (Sex that is too quick and only focused on penetration and orgasm can also lead to an avoidance of intimacy.)

Get out of Your Head and into Your Body

Another way to help you stay out of your mind and more centered in your body is to remember *there's nothing wrong with being aroused wherever you are.* We're not used to carrying arousal around with us throughout the day; sometimes we feel shame from being turned on (especially if it's at, say, a coffee shop or the office). But for better sex, you need to embrace and encourage your own sexual energy. Allow it to exist and carry it with you.

If you are turned on at work, or by someone you see at the gym, or by a random fantasy, take that sexual energy home and engage your partner with it. Use it to sext your partner from the office. Or use it to work out harder. Let your sexual energy and arousal be a motivator, and remember that not all sex needs to culminate in release or orgasm.

Play More

One way to stop focusing on orgasm so much is to actively practice making sex about play and fun—a zigzaggy, unguided exploration instead of a rote formula.

When kids play together, they're spontaneous. They don't usually have a set goal in mind. They just hang out, chase each other, draw pictures together, whatever. There's no overarching plan; they're just spending time together. When they're done, they leave.

In the bedroom, focusing on play should look more like focusing on the exploratory experience and less about the outcome. Maybe it's lying down, kissing each other, touching each other, and letting things go where they go.

The other piece involved in sexual play is breaking out of your usual formula. Many of us follow a standard protocol when we have sex: for a guy hooking up with a woman, it might look like kissing them, then touching their breasts, then touching their vaginas, then penetrating them. This kind of formula is the opposite of play. Instead of always allowing yourself to fall into this sex rut, try starting at step three and ending at step one. For instance, try starting off with oral sex and ending with making out. Try sex without any penetration, or even without incorporating the genitals!

You can also try using toys, role-play, sex games, and more to help break out of your usual patterns and have more fun.

Mixing up the steps challenges the flat, routine, patriarchal type of penetrative sex that dominates most of our ideas of what sex should look like. Play, touch, and socialization are the most important components for healthy brain development, intimacy, and happiness, and sex is one of the most powerful ways to accomplish all these things. Our culture's lack of emphasis on play is part of why so many adults don't know how to be in relationships, have good sex, or have happy lives. Play teaches all of this: it helps us find creativity and value in simply pursuing pleasure.

"AM I GAY IF . . . ?"
(OR "IS MY BF/GF GAY IF . . . ?")

One of the questions people ask me most often is whether enjoying a finger or toy in their butt means they're "gay." Um, in a word, no. Our culture's obsession with gender norms and with men's maintenance of traditional masculine standards, which demand avoiding anything "effeminate," makes it challenging for people to feel fully comfortable in their desires—especially if those desires involve butt play.

First, anything a heterosexual-defined person does is heterosexual, period. Everyone gets to define their sexual orientation for themselves. Few are exclusively hetero. And recent studies show that up to 56 percent of millennials don't define themselves as hetero; they identify as bisexual, fluid, gay, nonidentified, heteroflexible, or queer.

Now, back to things in your butt. No one gets pregnant from anal! Yes, people with a prostate are able to have more arousal and better orgasms from anal stimulation, but people without prostates can experience tons of pleasure there, too, because the anus is a highly innervated body part. The pelvic floor area—the area around your urethral area, around your vagina or penis, and all the way down and around your anal area—is full of networks of super-sensitive, arousal-inducing nerves. Anal for everyone!

Enjoying anal play or anal sex doesn't make someone "gay"—the notion that it does is homophobia at its worst! It just makes them sexually confident, a fun partner, and full of hot orgasms. If you want to try anal play with your partner but aren't sure where to start, this should help.

Preparation for anal sex is about more than cleanliness or hygiene; it's also about relaxing and being comfortable. Few people have taken the time to touch, look at, or play with their anus because culturally we see this area as dirty, but that's a big myth.

- **PREP FOR ANAL BY TALKING ABOUT IT OPENLY.** Make it less taboo by discussing it with partners and friends. Lots of people are curious about anal play and lots have engaged in it. Find out what it was like for them.

- **RELAX.** Be as physically comfortable as possible before you start any sort of anal play (alone or with a partner). It makes the encounter infinitely more pleasurable and sexy.

- **TOUCH YOUR ANAL AREA, LOOK AT IT, AND PLAY WITH IT.** Do this often! Get used to the experience of your butt being associated with pleasure.

- **MASTURBATE WHILE STIMULATING YOUR ANUS.** This is a great way to start associating it with orgasm and overall good stuff. (Always use short, manicured nails if you're engaging in anal play with your fingers.)

- **TRY OUT SOME TOYS.** Experiment with toys and small flexible dildos (only ones made for the butt, meaning they have a flared base so they can't get stuck). This helps train your anus for pleasurable insertion.

- **USE LUBE.** The anus and rectum are able to handle the insertion of a finger, toy, or penis safely, but using lube—and slow initial movements—is important, because anal tissue is more delicate than vaginal or mouth tissue.

- **COMMUNICATE WITH YOUR PARTNER THE ENTIRE TIME.** Enjoyable anal requires sharing what feels good or less than good while being penetrated; asking your partner if they're aroused while you're penetrating them; and continually reapplying lube.

BREAK OUT OF YOUR SEX RUT: A CHECKLIST

- When and where do you normally have solo and partnered sex?
- Where on your body and theirs do you typically touch, and in what order? (genitals only? full body? first kissing, then breast touching, then penetration?)
- What positions do you have solo sex in? (sitting, standing, lying, etc.)
- Do you use fantasy and porn?
- Do you always orgasm or make orgasm the goal?
- Do you always have penetration or make penetration the goal?
- Do you use toys or simply engage with genitals?
- Do you keep the lights on or off?
- Do you make eye contact, or do you have sex in positions in which you can't see each other?
- Do you kiss?
- What do you do after orgasm?
- Do you make sounds? (loud, quiet, silent, etc.)
- Do you move or stay still?
- Do you take shallow breaths or deep, long breaths?

SEVEN STEPS FOR YOUR BEST SEX EVER

1. Have no goal! Have nowhere to go and nothing to do, and don't force orgasm or penetration.
2. Pay attention to your body: focus on how it feels. Be *present* (use eye contact and touch).
3. Focus on yourself.
4. Go slow and relax; force nothing.
5. Be creative: avoid old habits, explore new things, and have no rules.
6. Make sounds, move around, breathe, and be messy.
7. Ask: give voice to what you want and be active.

Both Your Brain and Your Body Need New Experiences to Grow Sexually

Our brains are ever evolving and hyper-associative, allowing for new experiences of arousal all the time. Every time you experience something new in bed, your brain and your arousal levels grow. This means that being open to new sexual experiences can lead to serious expansion when it comes to your sex life. Too much consistency deadens your brain's capacity for growth, so don't let yourself get stagnant. Novelty is a good thing. Some things you didn't like when you were younger—for example, having your toes sucked or your hair pulled—can be super-erotic later in life.

Don't forget my rule of *not knocking it until you've tried it at least three times.* Great sex allows for a multitude of sexual experiences, including those that may push you outside the boundaries of who you thought you were. Some of these new pathways may be confusing; others may be highly arousing. If we remain open to newness, our sexualities will expand and incorporate a wealth of fresh pleasure triggers. This is how sex can be kept fun and novel, which are the keys to high desire.

Our sex lives often become too reliant on comfort and consistency. This can cause us to engage in sex that feels comfortable and familiar but isn't necessarily hot or exiting. Yet our arousal systems are plastic and malleable.

If you feel safe and trust your partner, try something new in bed (or out of bed!), and try it at least a few times to fully explore your response to it.

What follows are some ideas for new practices you can try incorporating with your partner, or on your own. Again, if it's not your thing, that's totally fine. They're just ideas! See what resonates with you, and try pushing yourself past your comfort zone.

Adding Someone Else to the Mix

Threesomes can be a great way to add a dose of sexual excitement to a happy, stable relationship, *happy* and *stable* being the key words here. My general rule: if you're having trouble in your primary relationship, it's not the time to try anything potentially complicated, like inviting someone else into your bedroom. Otherwise, you risk introducing feelings like jealousy and self-doubt ("Why'd she make that face when he was going down on her? She never made that face with me!"). It's when your relationship is smooth sailing that you've got the trust and commitment required to enjoy something like a threesome.

If your relationship is solid and you're both on board with bringing in a third party for a night, make it a priority to discuss exactly what you want to have happen. What are you both comfortable experiencing? What are you not comfortable with? Now's the time to set some expectations and boundaries: yes to oral, no to anal, whatever you agree on.

Arrange a safe word or a phrase you'll both agree to say during the encounter if you need to stop. Having this safety net will help you both feel more secure during the main event. Remember, this sexual encounter with a third person is still mainly about your primary relationship; it should bring you closer together. It's not about leaving anyone out; it's about experiencing a new person together as a strong, bonded unit.

Next, you need to find someone to invite into the fold. I suggest initiating three-ways only with someone you don't know, because when you're having a threesome, you're building intimacy. There *is* connection there; it's not always just sex. If you do it with a friend or even an acquaintance, there's the potential to change how you relate to that person every day (not to mention adding more complexity to your primary relationship).

I recommend using a dating app to look for a suitable threesome partner. Try creating a shared profile that you and your partner can both access, which features both of your photos and presents you as a unified front soliciting this experience together. Be honest, clear, and direct about what you're looking for. Write something like "We're in a primary relationship. We're not looking for someone to date, but we are looking for someone to join us for a one-night-only threesome." You don't want to mislead potential partners, and no one can adequately consent to sex unless they know exactly what's on the table.

After the main event, talk about it with your partner in detail: "How was it for you? Is there anything you would do differently next time?"

What if the idea of having a threesome—or doing something else in bed—turns your stomach? That's fine! I support the idea of using sex to increase intimacy with a partner, but no one should engage in acts that make them feel unsafe. Healthy relationships and sexuality require both honesty and compassion. The act of telling a partner that a sexual behavior is off-limits for you is practicing healthy communication; it's effectively telling them, "I care about you, so I want you to learn this about me." How a partner responds to being told "no" lets you see how healthy they are and how compatible you are together. You need to be direct and confident when you turn down a request for a particular act, but try to offer an alternate idea so the sex can keep going (and stay hot). "No, I'm not into that, but I *would* be turned on by . . ."

CLIENT CASE STUDY

I once worked with a client I'll call "Daryl." One day, Daryl's fiancée, a lawyer, unceremoniously freaked out after snooping on his computer and uncovering some colorful varieties of porn. She sent him to see me to help "straighten him out," assuming that there was something pathologically wrong with him simply because of the type of erotic imagery he enjoyed (which was perfectly legal, by the way). When Daryl came to see me, I reassured him that he was free to have a solo sex/fantasy life that belonged to him and him alone, one that was private and beyond his future wife's purview. (We're all entitled to that.)

After working with him for a while, I was astounded— in a good way—to see his relationship turn around. Why? Because Daryl began to understand and internalize the truth: *that he had nothing to be ashamed of.* It wasn't fair for his partner to hold him accountable for his masturbatory life, and when he truly believed this and began asserting this to his fiancée, their dynamic brightened by leaps and bounds. After opening the lines of communication in their relationship, his self-worth grew, she respected him more, and their partnership slowly but surely improved. It wasn't like things magically changed overnight. They both had to commit to pushing themselves for the sake of the relationship, and Daryl's fiancée actually came in to see me privately, as well, to help her learn to accept and respect the new person in front of her. Overall, porn was the trigger topic that helped Daryl revamp his self-esteem, which in turn helped him build his relationship skills and sexual confidence.

Role-Play

Some people find great pleasure in acting out sexual scenes—from fantasies, porn, books, or movies. If that's you, great! If you're not sure you're into it, perhaps it's worth a try.

If you want to role-play but can't think of any specific ideas, consider acting out a scene from a movie or TV show you both like (either XXX stuff or regular fare). But remember: the purpose of role-play is arousal. This means you need to understand what turns your partner on.

Don't go overly stereotypical when you're thinking about trying role-play; don't immediately assume a scenario like "naughty teacher" is hot for everyone (for some people that might read as corny). *Talk to your partner about what images and scenarios turn them on.* Ask what they fantasize about.

Of course, not everyone will enjoy role-play. Just as not all guys are tops and not all women are bottoms, not everyone can effectively role-play in the bedroom. Personally, I don't have it in me; I'm a horrible actor, so it's not believable and it's not hot for the other person. I don't know how to pretend I'm a masseuse; sorry, I've tried!

One way to help fire up your imagination is *going to sex boutiques as a couple.* Find a sex shop (either in your town or online) that sells various costumes and props. Go with your partner, explore together, and weigh in about what turns you on. Not only are you sharing the experience of finding the right gear, but even just walking around together, touching the clothes, and discussing ideas can be a turn-on in and of itself. Just like when you watch porn together, you'll stumble on things you may have never considered before that, lo and behold, are incredibly charged for both of you. You'll learn all about each other's unique arousal template.

Remember, too, that role-play involves all the senses. Notice what you're smelling and hearing. Put on different music. Try burning candles, lighting a fireplace, changing up the lighting. All our senses can heighten and enhance sex. And be sure to talk about it with your partner afterward. *Role-play is a fun, experimental game of trial and error.* After you wrap up, talk to your partner openly about what you did and didn't like. Discuss ways to do it differently next time.

Sex Toys

Toys like dildos, vibrators, masturbation sleeves, prostate stimulators, and butt plugs can be a good way to add excitement and novelty to your relationship. But there are a few important things to remember if you're interested in incorporating toys into your routine (on your own or with a partner).

CHECK OUT THE SAFETY OF THE MATERIALS. Some plastic toys contain unsafe chemicals like phthalates. You don't want those. You're potentially putting these objects inside you (or inside someone else)—find products without icky stuff in them!

CLEAN YOUR TOYS AFTER EACH USE, WHETHER YOU USE THEM ALONE OR WITH A PARTNER. You can also use condoms on inserted toys to help keep them clean, but you should still wash them off afterward.

STRETCH YOUR LIMITS, BUT ALWAYS BE SAFE AND AWARE. Don't try anything new that sounds dangerous to you, or if you're messed up on drugs or alcohol. You might not be able to set boundaries, assess pain, or take proper care of yourself and others.

IF YOU'RE IN A LONG-TERM RELATIONSHIP, EXPERIMENT! Push your boundaries with a toy you might be a little freaked out by. (Obviously, don't do anything you actively dislike or are afraid of, but challenge yourself here and there.)

STEP OUTSIDE YOUR USUAL OR ASSUMED ROLES. Sex toys aren't just for women! Dudes can enjoy toys in their butt, too. The whole body is a place to play. Try using sex toys like vibrators on a guy partner—vibrators can feel great anywhere, from the penis to the balls to the area between the butt and balls. Think beyond standard gender roles!

SEXT TO STAY CONNECTED

One of the biggest ways of keeping your relationship hot is to keep sexualizing each other on a day-to-day basis. This means complimenting your partner, touching them, leaving them sexy notes, and, of course, sexting them.

Sexting is fun. It's also a legit form of sex all on its own, and it can be an amazing way to build your sexual rapport with a partner when you're apart. But when it comes to sexting, always consider your audience. While nudity isn't inherently harmful—obviously I think we should all be naked more often!—sending unsolicited genital pics to someone you don't have a sexual relationship with can be intrusive and problematic.

Remember consent and compassion: my two fundamental rules, which also apply to sexting. Sure, I've sent dick pics, but not as a sneak attack on someone I've just met. When someone sexts you, honor the reason they sent the pictures to you: to turn you on and build intimacy. Then *delete the photos.* If you want to sext someone but you feel weird about it, crop your face out, as well as other distinguishing features.

Sexting is supposed to arouse, so make it sexy. It's a learned skill, and may take some practice (you may need to ask what kind of pics your partner is into). For example, once I was sexting with someone who kept sending me photos that looked staged and overly polished. So I asked, "Hey, do you have anything more natural looking?" The person got upset, but when I explained that their idea of sexy wasn't necessarily *my* idea of sexy, it clicked. What's hot isn't universal.

Dear Dr. Chris,

My new boyfriend has a small penis. I love him and everything else is going great between us, but I'm having a hard time getting into sex with him because I don't feel strong enough sensations when he's actually inside me. What can I do?

DR. CHRIS: Penis size is a loaded topic, so you'll need to be sensitive in how you address this with your boyfriend. You definitely don't want to criticize his penis size for being "less than"; that's body-shaming and it's not cool. This would be the same as criticizing a woman for having cellulite or small boobs. And just like it's okay to have cellulite, it's okay to be born with a smaller penis. Your boyfriend surely has other fun body parts for you to enjoy, and he can happily pleasure you with the trifecta of fingers, tongue, and toys. Also, penis extenders actually exist now—they're a special tool that can add length and girth during sex. Something like this could potentially help you if you need more sensation during the act. Just be sure to broach the topic sensitively, and don't force any kind of tool or toy on him if he's not into it.

CHECKLIST OF THINGS TO EXPLORE ALONE OR WITH A PARTNER (EXPLORE WHAT TURNS YOU ON!)

Anal

Cyber sex

Strip tease

Exhibitionism

Fantasy play

Vaginal fisting

Anal fisting

Gender play

Group sex

Three-ways

Swinging

Partner swapping

Erotic massage

Role-play

Outdoor sex

Toys

Phone sex

Sexting

Skype sex

Double penetration

Fantasizing about sex with others or friends

Pee play

Foot play

Anilingus (rimming)

69-ing

Voyeurism

Watching porn

Making homemade porn

Sharing homemade porn with others

BDSM (bondage, discipline, sadism, masochism) practices such as tying up your partner; getting tied up

Blindfold play

Whipping

Wrestling

CHAPTER 8 WRAP-UP

ASK YOUR PARTNER TONS OF QUESTIONS—
AND MAKE ZERO ASSUMPTIONS ABOUT
THEIR TURN-ONS.

SLOW DOWN!

INCORPORATE YOUR FULL BODY INTO YOUR
SEXUAL PLAY AND INTERACTIONS.

IGNORE GENDER ROLES.

MIX THINGS UP AND GET CREATIVE—ABOUT
WHEN YOU DO IT, WHERE YOU DO IT, AND
HOW YOU DO IT.

DON'T MAKE ORGASM THE GOAL.

THERE SHOULD BE NO ULTIMATE AIM EXCEPT
PLEASURE, CONNECTION, AND PLAY.

BE FREE TO TALK (ASK AND GUIDE), MAKE
SOUNDS, BE MESSY, AND USE MOVEMENTS
(DON'T BE STILL!).

SHARE YOUR FANTASIES.

STAY IN YOUR BODY, NOT YOUR HEAD

Most people live their entire lives in their heads. We question; we judge; we analyze; we worry; we overthink. We find it hard to unplug and stop the hamster wheel of what-ifs. And while our brains play a huge part in nearly everything we do and believe, thinking too much and being too "in your head" will *not* help your sex life.

In fact, if you want hot, happy sex, you need to make a commitment to get out of your brain and into your body. This chapter will touch on the mind-body connection and how it comes into play in your sexuality and relationships (as we've mentioned before, healthy sex doesn't involve only your genitals; in fact, it may not even involve them at all).

Get in Touch

Regardless of gender, our entire bodies have the capacity to experience pleasure. Allowing ourselves to feel it doesn't always come easily, though. Many of us have what I call *pleasure amnesia*. It's not that our bodies don't have the capacity to feel pleasure; it's that they've been socialized *away from it* because we're encouraged to ignore entire erogenous zones on our bodies. This can happen because of internalized shame, as well as external factors like religion, gender socialization, homophobia, and the sex- and body-negative family values we're raised with. More pleasure in sex occurs only when we embrace and legitimize more pleasure in other areas of our lives.

The more we touch and explore our bodies—or ask someone else to touch and explore them, per our direction—the more we can learn about all the varieties of pleasure that are available to us. You can't separate your body from your brain, or your brain from your body: they are interconnected and each affects the other. Your brain is what sends the final signal for genital arousal, and when your mind is anxious or unrelaxed, your body will follow suit, which will shut down your arousal. A tense, anxious mind leads to tense, anxious genital response.

We can't have great sex or sustainable, happy relationships until we've learned how to fully embrace our own pleasure: both the sexual and nonsexual kinds. How can we do this? We have to *get into our bodies and out of our heads.*

Physical touch can help, but sadly, many of us today are painfully starved of physical touch. We stumble through our days forgetting the powerful sense of comfort that can be derived from a simple hug or kiss. We *need* human touch—it strengthens neurological connections between our bodies, brains, and genitals. It also helps wake up specific neural networks and shakes us out of pleasure amnesia. (Lack of touch, or even simply avoiding one area of the body, actually weakens that area's capacity for pleasure.) Sex, pleasure, and touch are vital parts of our nervous system's development and health, and not just in a sexual context. Everyone gets to decide what role pleasure will take in their life; it's on you to get your neurology and nervous system more geared toward pleasure and healthy sexuality.

Here are a few of my preferred ways of helping you get back into your body and experience the pleasure of connecting with your own pleasure.

Full-Body Touch

We relate to ourselves, our sexualities, and others with our bodies. Mass culture is neither sex- nor body-positive, so we have to develop sex and body positivity on our own; we can't wait for the outside world to make us feel safer. The thing is, you can't be fully inside your body if you're anxious about *any* of your body parts or functions. And sex negativity, which is a form of sexual trauma, can actually get held and stuck in our body, then expressed in our sexuality and genitals. Sex phobia can actually become embedded as part of our nervous system.

I'm a huge proponent of full-body touch as a tool to help boost our capacity for tactile pleasure. Full-body touch (such as massage) integrates *all* our compartmentalized body parts and removes the associations of "good" parts and "bad" parts. It can help heal old relational wounds and body shame by showing us that our entire body is actually good, because the *entire body* has the capacity for pleasure. Healthy sex and relationships are about integration and wholeness—incorporating the entire body and allowing various kinds of healthy touch and exploration to occur.

Your self-esteem is closely tied to how you feel about your body, including your genitals. Avoiding certain parts of your body or associating them with pain, shame, or fear can hinder intimacy and thus prevent you from having awesome sex. Even hiding your body in oversized clothes can be a sign of body shame; why should we hide who we are under a veil of modesty? Working through your sex and body shame may mean having sex that at times causes you to feel slightly anxious. This is because you're pushing yourself toward more intimacy and vulnerability.

Massage is a great way to ease into different sorts of arousal and body acceptance. I advocate massage that includes the genitals because touch that *avoids* the genitals reinforces the message that they are bad and should be avoided. Even if the masseuse or your partner isn't touching your genitals, you might find yourself getting turned on, which is perfectly natural and great. Acknowledging this will help you learn how to absorb and experience *all* sensations of pleasure, no matter where it occurs on your body and no matter where it leads. You don't have to reach orgasm to feel amazing.

Massage and other touch that allows for full-body engagement (including the genitals) is incredibly powerful for precisely this reason: it helps you find a broader sense of full-body pleasure, and it encourages people to remember that their genitals aren't bad or dirty, and neither is being turned on.

Knowing the anatomy of arousal and orgasm is important because so few of us are supported in prioritizing pleasure. The work is about unlearning the limits placed on sexual exploration. Through body work like massage, new pathways to pleasure are opened up, and new body parts can become eroticized.

Dance, yoga, and movement therapies can also help you get more in touch with your body and learn about the ways your entire body is linked to pleasure and joy.

The Power of Pleasure

Often when I ask patients how they *feel*, they tell me what they are *thinking*; this is how cut off many of us are from our bodies. The real work is in feeling our own bodily sensations, both during sex and in other parts of our lives. You can't access pleasure through simply talking or thinking, and being disconnected from our bodies can also separate us from the people we love.

We may tend to think of pleasure as a secondary feeling that's outside us, but the capacity for it is actually hardwired within our brains. We all deserve regular, mind-blowing forms of pleasure, both sexual and nonsexual.

My biggest suggestion is simple: *stop dissociating from your body while you're getting busy!* Remember, good sex is about getting out of your head and into your body—"bottom up," as I call it. *Using* your body is not the same thing as being *inside* your body. Being disembodied and dissociated during sex only encourages fear and diminishes your own satisfaction. It causes you to check out and not feel present.

This dissociation can occur due to low intimacy tolerance, body shame, past sexual trauma, and other factors. Signs of dissociation include having sex with one's eyes closed, always keeping the lights off, and preferring genitals-only fast sex that neglects the rest of the body. People who dissociate may feel that sex makes them too vulnerable, so they mentally check out.

Avoiding sex can also be a form of dissociation; it's a distancing from your body and physical sensations. But when you focus on how sex *feels* instead of thinking of it as an orgasm-driven task—or overthinking how you might feel or look to your partner—your sexual experience will be infinitely better. Staying in your body and in your feelings during sex can also help you build a more mindful, connected relationship. And when you learn how to focus primarily on pleasure during sex, you can learn to legitimize pleasure in other areas of your life.

To help you stay present in your body, not your head, try regularly checking in with yourself during sex. Ask yourself how your body feels and exactly what you feel like doing next: "How does this *feel* to me? What do I want—from my partner or myself—*right now*? Is there something I could be doing to help me enjoy and embrace this experience even more?"

This helps stop the cycle of sexual disembodiment or the sensation of "checking out." If sex, for you, is often about being passive or having things done *to you*, focusing more on how you feel and what you want would probably benefit you, while also discouraging dissociation. Experiment with taking a more active role; show your partner what feels good and ask them what they like. Breathe. Ask lots of questions. Try new things. Feel, experience, and say what's happening inside you.

And remember, all bodies are wired and innervated differently. We all carry different forms of sex and body shame, as well as varying levels of sexual confidence. You can't assume that what worked for your last partner will work for someone else; every time you have sex with someone, it's an entirely new experience. As discussed in previous chapters, an intersectional lens reminds us that someone's level of privilege and oppression will have a deep impact on their capacity for being fully embodied and feeling safe with sex partners.

Feeling empowered to ask for what you want sexually may not be easy for everyone and can be more difficult—or simply different—for those with a minority identity (essentially, anyone who doesn't identify as white, cis, thin, able-bodied, attractive, upper middle class, or hetero: anyone who falls under an "ism"). Your body and sexual anatomy hold your trauma, which can be triggered through racism, body shame, homophobia, transphobia, and so on. Take steps to help yourself heal because sex shouldn't just be good—it should be great.

CLIENT CASE STUDY

A cis hetero couple came in to see me a few years ago. They'd been together for about a year and said they had reasonably good sex, but the boyfriend—"Malcolm"— refused to go down on his girlfriend ("Jeannie"). He had literally never done it, although she'd told him many times that it was an integral part of what helped her get off. His rationale for skipping out? He'd had one bad experience. He claimed the woman he'd been with before Jeannie had mocked him for not being "good" at oral, and somehow, in Malcolm's mind, it became a roadblock he couldn't get past with any woman, no matter how much he adored her.

This is what I said to Malcolm and what I'd say to anyone else with similar sexual hang-ups: we all have issues. But your anxiety about going down on Jeannie is all centered on your past experiences—your baggage. Also, as men, we're taught certain (false) things about which body parts are okay to engage with and which sexual practices are safe for "real" men to take part in. Some men claim they don't go down on women because they feel it lessens their masculinity or shows passivity or weakness, which is obviously a ridiculous argument.

When you say, "I won't allow certain parts of my body to be touched" or "I won't touch a certain part of my partner's body," you're blocking intimacy, because none of these activities are going to harm you.

Going down on your girlfriend will only bring you closer, make her happier, and strengthen your connection. It's clean, it's hygienic, it's safe, and it can be fun for both of you. In Malcolm's case, it took some pushing over the course of a couple of sessions before he was ready to try oral with Jeannie. They built up to it slowly, and with a bit of practice—and through seeing how much she enjoyed herself—he came to enjoy it and practice it regularly as part of their sexual repertoire.

This Is Your Brain on Relationships

We aren't static and our brains aren't, either. This is called neuroplasticity: our brains' unique ability to reorganize and form new connections in response to new situations, people, and environments.

Neuroplasticity allows us to heal after painful transitions; if you've ever gone through breakups or other challenging relational experiences—whether with family, friends, lovers, or whomever—your brain has changed as a result. It's why I emphasize dating and having sex with compassion: sexual relationships lend us the power to either heal or wound our partners.

It might sound like a cliché, but relationships change us, both in body and mind. *All* our experiences affect our brains and our bodies on a concrete level. During a relationship, diverse sexual and relational experiences actually help *boost the health of our brains*. In many ways, maintaining neuro (aka, brain) health is the same as maintaining relational and sexual health: the keys are fluidity, adaptability, and openness. Rigid mind = rigid body = rigid sexuality = bad sex. Opening up to a full range of sensations in your body will help your brain do the same. It's a feedback loop; because your body, brain, and emotions are all interconnected, a shift in one creates a shift in the others.

Love, especially, builds and changes our brains. In fact, love actually stems from the brain: lust, attraction, and attachment are all linked to chemicals and hormones, which are sent ricocheting through our systems when we're in different phases of a relationship. When you are falling in love, your brain will naturally start to associate your partner with pleasure and joy. The more you build these positive associations, the more you're deepening and strengthening your relationship, and the better the relationship will be. You'll start to crave that positive pleasure association you have with your partner, and you'll both start to become dependent on each other for pleasure. With healthy intimacy, you'll allow yourself to be vulnerable and present. The more time you spend with your partner and the more intimacy you have—meaning physical touch, eye contact, and connected sex—the stronger your neuro health will be.

Of course, the opposite is also true: if you and your partner fight all the time or experience triggers that lead to romantic discord, you may start associating your partner with negative feelings and emotions.

Our sexual likes, needs, and dislikes will morph over time, but opening yourself up to new sexual sensations will help improve your brain *and* keep your relationship hot and exciting. Yup, I'm telling you that openness in bed can actually improve your mental health.

Your Brain on a Breakup

When you go through a breakup—or any kind of major transition—in a relationship, there will be identity loss. You're forced to shuffle your own self-perception and ask yourself some tough questions: "I'm single now—what does that mean? Who am I without my partner?" But there's also a neurological rupture. The relationship you were in changed your brain and your body. And if your partner's presence regularly generated feelings of happiness, connection, and closeness, those feelings are now gone. No wonder relationship transitions hurt so much!

You can't ignore or hide your injury; this is a crucial time to master the art of self-care. Treat yourself as if you're physically sick, because you are neurologically needing healing. It's okay to take off work if you need to. Focus on self-care: activities that nourish you and make you feel better. You'll probably experience sadness, and that's fine. Recovery will require rewiring everything, including your emotionality and how you feel socially. As a society, we need to find a way to be more sensitive during breakups (both our own and other people's), because many of our physical and biological systems need to find a new equilibrium during those times.

How can you stabilize and move on? Through novelty. Let's say a person goes through a really bad breakup and they feel miserable, lonely, and depressed. Instead of doing the same activities they've always done, they push themselves to start hanging out in different neighborhoods, doing different things and going to new events to expand their social circles. Though it might feel uncomfortable and difficult at first, they slowly begin to make new friends—and bring a new sense of joy and wonder into their lives. The new friendships and relationships they're forming help distract them with new thoughts and activities. They're reminded that they're fun, interesting, and desirable. Sure, they might not be 100 percent back to their old self, but now there's a *new self*, and a new understanding of who they are and what the future can look like without their ex.

Of course, most people don't follow that advice. They do the opposite. They hide out and wallow in the breakup, because that's what feels most comfortable. Push yourself past your comfort zone in times of romantic distress—seek out newness. Going out and being social is a great way to distract yourself, but more important, it helps reorganize your brain in a positive way. You get to create new experiences to help fill that old emotional void and find fresh sources of pleasure again.

Dear Dr. Chris,

I dated the same person for eight years and we recently broke up after a long, painful, stagnant period during which we didn't have sex for months. Although our relationship was no longer happy or sexually fulfilling, I really miss having someone to share my day-to-day life with. I feel totally depressed and isolated. What can I do to move on?

DR. CHRIS: I know it feels excruciating right now, but remember, a breakup is simply a change in your relationship; it isn't a death sentence. Your brain and your heart will adapt to this new reality and your identity will shift, too. But if you want to start feeling better faster, take some proactive steps ASAP to help you regain your emotional footing. First, get back in touch with your own sexuality. Just because you didn't have a lot of sex with your partner doesn't mean you can't change that now. Masturbate more. Seek out new relationships, hookups, and flings, if you feel inspired. Remind yourself that you're sexy and desirable, and remember how fun sex with someone new can be!

Also try visiting new coffee shops, restaurants, bars, and galleries. The key is to seek out places you've never been and expose yourself to people you've never seen. Now is the perfect time to do something you've always thought about doing, like planning a faraway vacation, taking a class in something you've never done before, getting involved in activist work, writing a book, or learning a new sport. Push yourself to expand your own self-definition. Remember that you're a new version of yourself, but that doesn't mean this new version of you is any less valuable, worthy, or desirable than the one that was in a relationship.

Reprogramming Your Brain

Because your body, brain, and psychology are all interconnected, a shift in one creates a shift in the others. Reprogramming your brain is about creating new, healthy habits—seeking out positive, healthy relationships and stronger personal connections that will wire you to *want* more touch, better sex, and stronger connections. Many of us unconsciously continue to reinforce sexual problems by not challenging our sexual habits and comfort zones.

You break old patterns when you allow new ways of sexual functioning within your body. Our patterning is so strong that we need to use our nervous systems and plenty of repetition to make changes stick. To build and strengthen new neural pathways and undo old ones requires uncovering new ways of being and doing, which can be uncomfortable. This is why we fight so hard to stick to our old habits and routines, even when they're not necessarily serving us. This is why reprogramming your brain and changing your sex life takes practice—you need to practice being different and learn how to become more sex- and body-positive moment by moment, encounter to encounter. Get rid of cultural conditioning, especially based on your gender, and open yourself up to full-body arousal and genital relaxation.

Your Body Holds Your Trauma

Sexual healing is a real thing. Your body and your sexual anatomy hold your trauma—we've all got trauma in some form, whether it's sexual abuse, childhood neglect, a violent relationship, or simply growing up in a toxic rape culture. Our traumas may quietly reveal themselves on our faces, in our body language, in our dating and sexual habits, and even in the way we carry ourselves: an inability to walk confidently or stand tall can be a sign of trauma. They are even reflected in how relaxed our genital areas are and how confident we are with sexual arousal and our sexual anatomy.

As I've touched on briefly above, all our past experiences and traumas are intertwined with our bodies and our minds. This is another reason it's so important to work on having fully present, embodied sex: you can start working on the issues that may be interfering with your capacity for amazing sex and fulfilling relationships. Sure, talk therapy is great, but talking can only take you so far; you have to actually do the physical work as well.

When you conform rather than being authentic, you ignore honest, in-the-moment experience. Let yourself have full sexual expression so you can use your body the way you'd like and fully express your sexuality.

CHAPTER 9 WRAP-UP

YOUR BRAIN IS CHANGING ALL THE TIME—
AND A LOT OF THESE CHANGES OCCUR
BECAUSE OF YOUR RELATIONSHIPS.

SEX MUST BE MINDFUL IN ORDER TO BE
MIND-BLOWING. DON'T "CHECK OUT"
DURING SEX—BRING YOURSELF BACK INTO
YOUR BODY. SLOW DOWN. BREATHE.

BREAKUPS ARE PAINFUL, BUT THEY'RE ALSO A
PRIME WAY TO HELP CREATE NEW PATTERNS
AND PUSH YOURSELF OUT OF YOUR
COMFORT ZONE TO TRY NEW THINGS.

PHYSICAL TOUCH IS IMPORTANT. FULL-BODY
TOUCH AND FULL-BODY MASSAGE CAN
HELP YOU CONNECT WITH YOUR BODY AND
YOUR SEXUALITY; OTHER THINGS TO TRY ARE
MOVEMENT THERAPIES, DANCE, AND YOGA.

LUST CAN'T LAST

"Why aren't we having sex anymore?"

"Where has my sex drive gone?"

These are two of the biggest clinical complaints people in long-term relationships approach me with—whether they're calling into my podcast or coming into my office. I understand why it feels disconcerting, even alarming, to realize that you're rarely having sex with your significant other. You still love each other, but things have changed. At the early stages of most relationships, everything is new and hot; it can feel like you're led around in a state of near-constant arousal and excitement. Every sexual experience feels passionate; you're getting it on all the time, trying new things, and seeing your partner through fresh eyes each day.

But eventually real life shows up: everything your partner does is no longer quite as cute, and having a "movie and cuddle" night every evening no longer seems as thrilling. This shift away from sexual heat and into the routines of everyday life is an incredibly common and somewhat inevitable stage of a monogamous relationship. Is it *fun*? Not necessarily—but it's also no reason to panic. Shift your perspective! Let it be more annoying than devastating, and commit yourself to becoming more sexually creative, inventive, and resourceful as a couple.

Sex is a powerful tool to maintain connection and intimacy in your relationship. The whole purpose of a primary partnership is just that: primary partnership. If you're not engaging in one of the main activities that bond you together, whether you're in a long-term monogamous relationship or a different type of relationship, you won't feel as close over time, and the fire may start to sputter even more. Then you could start to become resentful of your partner for appearing to reject this one powerful thing you've offered them and them alone: your sexuality and eroticism. You can't ask someone for monogamy but then be unwilling to prioritize sex.

Why Does Passion Decline in a Relationship?

There are various reasons why sex might start to dry up for people who have been together for a long time (monogamous or not).

The Thrill Is Gone

Whether it's a movie, a restaurant, or a sex partner, nothing is quite as viscerally exciting as something we've never seen, done, or experienced before. Think about it: it's just not as much fun to watch a movie you've watched fifteen times, right? And the more you go to the same restaurant, the more rote and mindless it becomes. You stop being quite as present to the food and the atmosphere. In some ways it's just . . . safe, like going through the motions. That's the same thing that can happen to your sex life throughout the course of a long relationship.

Let me illustrate with another example: when I used to run group therapies, I would tell my patients this funny story about how, when you get a new pair of shoes you're obsessed with, you think, "Oh my God—I'm never getting these babies dirty!" You clean off your shoes before you climb in the car; you avoid bumping into anything; you wear your shoes outside only in nice weather; you even wipe them off when you get home. But then somehow, magically, a couple of months later, someone accidentally steps on the toe of your beloved shoe and you think, "Whatever, no big deal." You stop caring quite so much that your "new" shoes are getting slightly dirty.

The more we get into a particular habit and the more comfortable we become with something—or someone—over time, the less care and attention we devote to it. What does this mean for our relationships? It might mean that our partners start to lose some of their luster; we don't treat them like a priceless new treasure anymore. I'll address ways to address these issues shortly.

You Feel Too Vulnerable

A lot of vulnerability exists in sexual expression. Sometimes it can almost feel too honest and intimate to share your authentic sexuality with someone—even someone you've known for a long time. What arouses you is one of the most private parts of yourself, and this can make it feel like it needs protection. The more attached you become to someone, the more their opinion of you begins to matter, and exposing fragile parts of yourself can make you feel more anxious. But failing to share what makes you anxious can actually cause your intimacy to stop and your relationship to function only on superficial levels. Not fun. Revealing *all* of your sexual self is an act of care and commitment.

Your Sex Drives Aren't Aligned

Another common element that causes couples to grow apart sexually is that they find, over time, that their sex drives simply aren't on the same level anymore. For instance, suddenly, after two years, a wife realizes she's typically the one initiating sex with her husband once a week—and that three times out of four, he rebuffs her advances because he's "tired." Or a couple finds one partner craving sex every other day, while the other person wants it just once a week.

This is incredibly common; often in low-sex relationships, one partner simply has a higher sex drive than the other and the two can't find common ground when it comes to how, when, and how often they want to get it on.

Of course, there's no right or wrong when it comes to sexual frequency; people's needs and desires are different. We all have different ideals when it comes to how often we crave carnality. Having a different libido than your lover doesn't have to be a deal breaker, but it's something you will need to work on together (keep reading for tips).

Something Is Off in the Relationship

Sometimes, the withering of the sexual aspect of a relationship *can* be a sign of an issue in the relationship, at least for one party. That's why seeing a sex-positive couples therapist is generally a win if the lack of intimacy persists. (See page 198 for information on finding a good therapist.)

There are plenty of other reasons why sex might start to fizzle out. Talk to your partner directly if you're concerned about your relationship; again, everyone is different.

Can Your Relationship Stay Happy—or at Least Afloat—If the Sexual Heat Has Subsided?

Of course, but it might be difficult. Our culture is so sexualized that we're constantly being bombarded with fresh stimuli. It's very hard *not* to compare your life and your relationship to whatever you see reflected around you, whether that's on social media, in ads, or in the general public. You are bound to find yourself in situations where you see someone attractive on the street and get hit with a primal wave of arousal. It's kind of like when you're out at a restaurant and you can't decide between the pizza and the pasta; after you've ordered the pasta, you glance over at the next table and notice someone fawning all over their pizza. Now what they have looks *sooooo* much better. We're biologically driven to compare this way, and it's only natural that we would do it with sex and relationships, too: "Oh my God, I miss that feeling. Why don't *I* have it anymore?"

Or you might see a cute young couple at a bar or coffee shop who can't keep their hands off each other, and again you're hit with a wave of longing: "Oh my God, I miss that. Oh my God, I want that back. Oh my God, we don't have that anymore."

And you might not. At least not right now.

Of course, there are some no-sex or low-sex relationships that still manage to stay happy, compatible, and close over the long haul. Often, in those relationships, both partners have a lower sex drive and both are fine with that. Those kinds of relationships are absolutely possible, and they're totally fine, if the partners are on the same page.

There are also long-term relationships in which the couples no longer feel that drive toward novelty, and instead they manage to find peace with the relationship as it is. It's like someone who grows up in their childhood home and ends up never leaving their home because it's comfortable, safe, and all they've really known. This phenomenon can absolutely happen in relationships—maybe two people have been having sex for decades and the sex is good enough. They're content with it. That's fine for them! But there are a lot of people who aren't content with the sexual aspect of their long-term relationship, and this chapter is more for them: the people who feel a bit restless or discontent or want to go deeper.

Of course, in any relationship, if both partners are on board with making changes, they can find ways to shift course—but both people must be willing to do the work and take the steps to find a happy sexual medium. Because even if your sex life is amazing and you're content, it's always possible to do more and make it better: to achieve greater authenticity and intimacy by doing the work to show your lover new sides of you. In order to do that, we must stop pursuing sex that's easy and habit based, and push ourselves past our sexual comfort zones. Great sex and happy relationships are about growing, evolving, and trying new things.

In some long relationships, partners don't grow anymore. They become flat, one-dimensional, closed off—not because their bodies are faulty but because they've stopped using sex and love to learn and grow. But just because the heat has dimmed doesn't mean the fire is dead.

Don't Be "Best Friends"

As a therapist, I frequently stumble across couples who have made the mistake of letting their romantic relationship veer too far in the direction of friendship. You know those couples who boast about being "best friends"? Sure, I get the appeal, but if you want a sexually healthy, stable romantic relationship, I'd advise you not to let your relationship move too far into the friend zone. Eroticize your partner regularly through flirting, sexting, touching, cuddling, and kissing; in other words, keep dating them. Even if you've been married for twenty years!

Your partner isn't just your friend. Let your friends be your friends. Of course, it's great if you can say that your lover happens to be your friend, too, but they should also be much more than that—they're your romantic partner, *romantic* and *partner* being the key words there. Unless you're asexual, your romantic partner should also be your *romantic sexual partner*. Which means your relationship should also include sex and romance. If it doesn't, own that—and work it back into your relationship, or you might just need to cut the cord and go find it with someone else. Or, if you see your partner as just a friend and no longer feel romantic or sexual feelings toward them, set them free and let them have a romantic and sexual connection with someone else. But don't deny them a crucial part of a relationship, because that's partly why you two are in a relationship.

How Can You Reignite the Sexual Flames?

Arousal is unpredictable, and it can't always fit into a neat box of the "right" time and place. Allow for the fluidity and spontaneity of desire within your relationship. The idea that something must be *wrong* if sexual interest shifts or drops during a relationship is dangerous; again, it's a natural outcome of monogamy, which is still the cultural gold standard. There are ways to keep it more fun and make sex better, but a decline in sexual interest is something most long-term partnerships will have to encounter and work with at some point.

If you find yourself in a position where the sexual flame seems to be dying and you want to turn things around, it's time to start initiating some (possibly uncomfortable) conversations. If you feel disconnected, lonely, or like you need more of something—anything—in your relationship, it's up to you to tell your partner that.

Start by *asking for sex to be a priority*. Tell your partner how attractive and desirable they are to you and how much you miss the sexual intimacy you once had in your relationship. Explain that you thrive on sexual connection and that you want it to be a bigger part of your life again. Complimenting them and emphasizing how hot you find them never hurts and is more likely to help them feel excited and connected to you.

Here are some other things to try to incorporate more sexuality into your relationship:

- All-day flirtation (sexy texts, photos, love notes, etc.) helps fuel and maintain desire.
- Novelty helps build desire: try new things, both in and out of the bedroom.
- Prioritize your relationship. Schedule time together as a couple, vacation together, and have date nights.
- Don't just say no if your partner wants to do something sexual; if you're not interested in the sexual activity they suggested, suggest something else sexual, sensual, or affectionate. This helps you stay connected.
- Stay in the relationship. Don't commit to someone and then just give up on attraction and flirtation. Relationshipping is an action: a practice you must actively choose to keep doing by staying present and engaged. You owe it to you and your partner to work at it.
- Don't make every night a Netflix night. Go on dates; get out of the house and do things. This helps breed novelty; you'll also get to see new sides of your partner.
- Experiment with watching porn together. (See page 153 for details.)
- Put down your phone when you're together. Looking at your phone in each other's company doesn't allow time for bonding (eye contact, touch, affection); in fact, it's an active blocker of connection and intimacy building. Leave phones out of the bedroom to allow space to connect and be sexual or affectionate. Stack them in a pile on the table when having dinner together.

- Take (and give!) a compliment. Your partner's expression of attraction for you is a gift and a move toward connection and intimacy. Enjoy and appreciate it when it happens. Don't forget to *give* compliments to your partner as well. Everyone likes to hear compliments, and they will remind your partner that you find them sexually desirable, which should in turn make them want to be sexual with you.
- You *can* have sex even when you're feeling a bit disconnected. In fact, it might actually help you reconnect. Sex shouldn't necessarily cease just because you're going through a rough patch.
- Use the four Cs: compliment, cuddle, care, and coevolve. The first two Cs are self-explanatory. Care means to watch the way you're communicating your needs to your partner; if you want something to change in the relationship, request it but don't criticize. Criticism is not sexy. Coevolve means to let yourselves grow together as a couple. Don't stop expanding and letting yourselves learn new things about each other.

If you're trying to stoke the sexual fires with your long-term partner, the key is to try things that are *new*. Examine what your gender typically demands (man is aggressive, woman is submissive, etc.) and do things *outside of that*. Push those boundaries. Examine what you personally already do sexually—and try something else. Use plenty of eye contact while you touch your partner. Be tender, even if you're a man! Men are not typically taught the importance of tenderness as children, so we have to learn it. Also try massages; give and get them with your partner regularly. These should be full-bodied massages that don't necessarily need to be sexual, but they'll likely be erotic.

Nonmonogamy for the Win?

If you want to stay in the relationship but are feeling stifled by sexual boredom, there *are* options. (And, no, cheating is not one of them.) As I've discussed throughout this book, nonmonogamy can be a solid approach to restrengthening your relationship's sexual foundation if long-term monogamy has started to kill your desire. For some couples, the *best thing* you can do for your relationship is to open it up to the possibility of other sexual connections.

What that might look like for you in the context of your own relationship is entirely your business. Maybe it's giving each other permission to go on dates outside the marriage; maybe it's having one or two one-night stands per year; maybe it's polyamory or maintaining other love relationships alongside your primary partner; maybe it's dabbling in an occasional threesome.

But whatever you decide, the critical element is communication: you must discuss your concerns and desires with your partner first. You need to come to an agreement about boundaries and parameters before any big change is made. If one person isn't on board, either work to find a compromise, drop it, or move on to a new relationship if that feels like the best option.

CLIENT CASE STUDY

A very smart, passionate, creative woman named "Monique" who'd been married to the same man for twenty years came to see me. She was incredibly annoyed by the fact that her husband regularly wanted to have sex with her. As if that was such an inappropriate, awful notion! She felt like he was pressuring her to "put out" when she didn't feel that intensity of desire for him anymore. I reminded her that no one expected her to have sex when she didn't actively want to; no one gets a pass to pressure, bully, or force their way into sex with a spouse. But again, finding yourself with mismatched sex drives over time is nothing to be alarmed about—it just takes some patience, time, and commitment, like every other aspect of a relationship. I reminded her that sex was a critical part of any romantic partnership, and that if she didn't feel like having sex with just her husband anymore, perhaps it was time to make a change and try something new. She asked her husband if he would be interested in "opening up" their marriage and having threesomes with another man every once in a while. Lo and behold, this did the trick and helped them steer into a happy new phase of their relationship. They both found entirely new types of pleasure, connection, and sexual fulfillment.

Dear Dr. Chris,

What do I do if my boyfriend never wants sex?

DR. CHRIS: This is an incredibly common question, and I know from experience it can feel triggering—like you're no longer attractive to your partner or that your needs are no longer important. Yes, sometimes being in a relationship will mean mourning the loss of the sex life you thought you would have (and had while you were single or first dating your partner). But again, for most long-term relationships, a lowered sex drive is part of long-term monogamous coupling. Again, familiarity is not as hot and sexy as newness. Tell your sig other how much you miss sex; discuss whether the sex you have is worth having (some sex just isn't that fun, so are you open to being more sexually diverse?) or in need of more creativity and possibly some kink (yes, I talk my long-term coupled patients who want more sexual energy into trying different kinks). Remember, you are more sexually fluid than you think and your true sexuality is far more diverse than even you realize or care to admit. What your partner does about your concern is a demonstration of what type of partner he is and how he will react when you discuss other aspects of the relationship that disappoint you.

Dear Dr. Chris,

What do I do with a partner who wants sex all the time?

DR. CHRIS: An always-horny partner can feel overwhelming to those with a lower sex drive or less sexual confidence (sexual anxiety, fear of sexting, or only enjoying one position). The solution is to be a caring, attentive partner. When your partner makes an attempt to connect, build closeness, and get off with you, do something sexual. If you're not up for penetrative sex, perhaps give oral or a hand job, use a toy, masturbate together, or watch porn, but find some way to engage with your partner in an intimate, pleasurable way. If you choose monogamy, it's not fair to force your partner into a life of celibacy.

When in Doubt, Find a Sex-Positive Therapist

If you find yourself resentful, frustrated, or at an impasse in a relationship where you're not seeing eye to eye about your sex life, try a sex therapist. But find a good one. A sex-positive therapist is a must. In our sex-shaming and sex-phobic culture, it's important to find a specialist who can provide a warm, open space for you to explore your creative sexuality openly. Differences are not disorders, and many traditional health care providers and therapists veer toward thinking that sexual health is about normalization and conformity rather than authenticity, self-acceptance, and sex positivity.

When you're in the market for a sex-positive therapist who supports sexual health, here are valuable questions to ask them:

1 *How many hours of training in human sexuality do you have?*
   Academia has done a poor job of educating mental health students in sexology, sex therapy, and human sexuality, with either no class requirements at all or sometimes only a pass/fail one-off class. Any training for sex-related therapy tends to be via specialized programs outside the university system. Some of them are good; some of them aren't. Find a therapist who is a certified sex therapist or has at least some hours of training in human sexuality under their belt.

2 *How do you feel about porn?* As I've mentioned, there is nothing wrong with porn, and in fact there can be therapeutic uses for porn. Like all forms of art, it has different capacities, and studies show that cultures with permissive attitudes toward sex and porn have fewer sex crimes, lower rates of teen pregnancy, and lower rates of STDs. Watching body-positive and female-gaze porn can increase body esteem for nonnormative bodies, help couples find new ways to be sexual, and more. The assumption that porn stars are broken victims is far from true.

3 *How do you feel about nonmonogamy and casual sex?* You were probably taught that sex is always between only two people in a monogamous relationship and that the main goal of sex and dating is to work toward marriage and reproduction. Today we know that's not for everyone and that healthy sex and relationships can be open, nonmonogamous, or poly. Open relationships can be just as much about fun and companionship as monogamous ones are, and they can be short-term with no commitments.

4 *Have you worked with trans clients?* Various gender presentations and diverse bodies exist, and not everyone's gender exists within the male/female binary. Most intake forms still offer only two options for gender, and most offices still have segregated bathrooms. Some clits are called dicks, and some men have vaginas and give birth. The real disorder is in seeing gender as solid and fixed, with a gendered brain, and in not challenging gender roles and gender norms (especially within sex, dating, and relationships). You might be wondering why this is important if you're not actually trans yourself. To that I would say a good sex-positive therapist should support diverse gender presentations, and if they don't, what other types of things might they be closed off to regarding your sexuality or sexual health?

5 *Have you worked with the LGBTQIA community?* A sex-positive therapist supports dating and sex with all genders, bodies, and sexualities. A therapist who supports sexual health has the ability to discuss nonpenetrative sex, sex with strap-ons, anal, fisting, PrEP (pre-exposure prophylaxis, anti-HIV medication that keeps HIV-negative people from becoming infected), sex apps, and same-sex parenting, and does not exhibit biphobia. Just as there is no common mind-set or common psychology among all heterosexual people, there is no "gay psychology" or "gay psyche" among gay people.

Intersectionality teaches us that no one leads a single-issue life. No one's identity should be reduced to being exclusively about their sexual attractions.

6 *Are there any types of sex you consider "dysfunctional"?* The mental health field still devalues sex as legitimate intimacy building ("have less sex," "wait to do it," etc.); it ignores the ways in which sex can be therapeutic and healing. Healthy sexuality is about a variety of options, including BDSM and kink. Sexual minorities do not need to honor puritanical definitions of how they "should" exist in the world to be seen as healthy.

7 *How do you define female sexual empowerment?* The suspicion toward anyone who enjoys sex openly, has a lot of sex, or prioritizes sex is so great that most of us immediately problematize sexual empowerment, especially for women, without any critical exploration. A healthy sex life can mean having as many sex partners as you want. There is no "correct" amount of sex or number of sex partners to have.

8 *What role does masturbation play in healthy sexuality?* Masturbation is one of the best ways to self-soothe, cope with difficult emotions and stress, and entertain oneself (or others). Daily masturbation is good for your psychology, your pelvic floor, and your mood. Sex and couples therapists should support it.

9 *Do you support the idea of more than two genders and self-identifications?* Not only is gender a (false) social construction, but gender norms and gender roles—along with concepts like a male and female brain—collapse complex and diverse ways of being into one monolithic identity. There are infinite genders, along with infinite labels, and all people get to decide for themselves. Your sex-positive therapist should understand this.

10 *Do you support bisexuality, asexuality, solosexuality, sexual fluidity, and fetish sexuality?* As a sex-positive therapist, I work with clients needing confirmation that it is okay to be asexual, solosexual, pansexual, fluid, and into objects rather than people, because not all of the mental health world recognizes that "difference is not a disorder." Similarly, your sex-positive therapist should support all sexualities.

11 *Do you use the "sex addiction" diagnosis or treatment model?* The "sex addiction" diagnosis has become a wastebasket for all nonnormative sexuality. I have worked clinically with many patients who spent years in sex addiction treatment, and our work becomes about deprogramming all the sex shame instilled in them. The sex addiction treatment model proposes all monogamous and hetero values as healthy sex and ignores other sexual norms and values (masturbation, porn, kink, hooking up, and sex for emotional regulation). The concept of sex addiction is sex-shaming, plain and simple.

Remember, lust may shift and change course a bit during a long-term relationship, but don't freak out. With a little patience and dedication, you can both find a new groove; just be sure to stay committed to finding new ways to keep your sex life (and your partnership) fresh. If both partners are willing to compromise, commit, and continue to care deeply about each other's pleasure, anything is possible.

CHAPTER 10 WRAP-UP

IT'S NORMAL FOR SEXUAL PASSION TO FADE OVER TIME. LET THIS BE MORE ANNOYING THAN DEVASTATING.

A DECLINE OF SEX IN A RELATIONSHIP IS NOT A DEATH SENTENCE, BUT YOU HAVE TO DO SOME WORK TO KEEP THINGS HOT.

DON'T BE "BEST FRIENDS" WITH YOUR PARTNER.

ASK YOUR PARTNER TO MAKE SEX A PRIORITY.

IF YOU ARE STILL STRUGGLING TO MAKE SEX A PRIORITY IN YOUR RELATIONSHIP, TRY A SEX-POSITIVE THERAPIST.

CONCLUSION

Relationships make up some of the most profound experiences of our lives. They can also be among the most chaotic and complicated. Living in a world where sex negativity and body shame bombard us on a daily basis can make it hard to live a life free from these triggers. Traditional, old-guard dating rules aren't harmless; they actually ignore various types of oppression while supporting the status quo.

Why follow these outdated rules? As I've explained in this book, sexual health is about celebrating—not repressing—our sexualities.

In a "faster, harder, more, now" culture, it's on us to work toward making our relationships the *opposite* of what we're traditionally taught—standard, "normal," boring, routine. What does the opposite look like? Not being goal focused or obsessed with appearance or performance; prioritizing intimacy and pleasure above all else. This is a rebellious and deeply needed act, because the ways in which most of us have been running our relationships are just *not working*. The game-playing, gender-policing, and meaningless rules of traditional dating fail us over and over again, keeping us trapped in outmoded systems that don't serve us.

Through intimacy and honest sexuality we can grow and learn more and more about ourselves. We can do this through more touch—more kissing, hugging, and obviously more sex—to make up for the ways our bodies have been shamed, devalued, and dismissed (sometimes by ourselves). Push yourself beyond your comfort zone, but respect people's boundaries. Stop slut-shaming yourself and others. Be intersectional in your thinking and your sexuality, and acknowledge how differences in gender, race, age, class, and more can create forms of privilege and oppression that play out in your relationships. Bringing this awareness into your individual sex life can actually help build a sexually healthy culture for everyone.

Sexual health means living from a more compassionate and evolved place where others can elevate their behavior to meet yours. This means asking for what you want, pursuing what truly excites you, and respecting what excites others (even if it doesn't work for you). Being the truest, most authentic version of yourself is ultimately what will transform you and your relationships—and eventually, maybe even the world.

ABOUT THE AUTHOR

Dr. Chris Donaghue PhD, LCSW, CST, is a therapist, lecturer, educator, and the author of *Sex Outside the Lines: Authentic Sexuality in a Sexually Dysfunctional Culture*. He is a licensed clinical therapist and certified sex therapist and sexologist, with a doctorate in clinical sexology and human sexuality. He is the director of clinical education for the Sexual Health Alliance (SHA) and is a member of the American Association of Sexuality Educators, Counselors, and Therapists (AASECT) and the Society for the Scientific Study of Sexuality (SSSS). He practices general psychology and specializes in individual and couples sex, relational, and marital therapy. His work also includes sexual and relational trauma work, sexual compulsivity, sexual anorexia, sexual dysfunctions, and nontraditional sexuality, identities, and relationships.

A highly requested speaker at prestigious universities, Dr. Chris has also served as keynote speaker at many professional conferences. He is cohost of the podcast *The Amber Rose Show with Dr. Chris* (formerly *Loveline*) and the host of the nightly radio show *Loveline with Dr. Chris*. He's also a weekly expert on *The Amber Rose Show,* a frequent cohost on *The Doctors*, and he was the host of WE TV's *Sex Box* and Logo TV's *Bad Sex*.

Dr. Chris has been featured on *The Today Show*, VICE, CNN, HLN, OWN, and *Nightline* and is regularly quoted and featured in national publications.

Dr. Chris's office is located in Los Angeles.